breaking the surface

breaking the surface

Sono
Nis
Press

VICTORIA B.C. CANADA

CANADIAN CATALOGUING IN PUBLICATION DATA

Breaking the surface

Poems

ISBN 1-55039-106-2

I. Canadian poetry (English)—20th century.*
PS8293.B686 2000   C811'.5408   C00-910262-0
PR9195.7.B73 2000

Sono Nis Press gratefully acknowledges the support of the Canada Council for the Arts and the Province of British Columbia, through the British Columbia Arts Council.

Cover and interior design by Jim Brennan
Cover photo by Jim Brennan
Copy edited by Dawn Loewen

Published by
Sono Nis Press
PO Box 5550, Stn. B
Victoria, BC V8R 6S4
tel: (250) 598-7807
sono.nis@islandnet.com
http://www.islandnet.com/sononis/

Printed and bound in Canada by Friesens Printing

ACKNOWLEDGEMENTS

Colebrook Peace: "Shadow Icarus" published in the *Antigonish Review*.

Cran: "Winter in a Seaside Home," "Death of a Friend by Overdose," and "Hitching" published in the chapbook *Songs I Used to Chase Rye* (Smoking Lung Press); "Roseau, Dominica" published in *Geist*; "Spider's 3 a.m." and "Patterns of Leaves" published in *Hammer & Tongs: A Smoking Lung Anthology* (Arsenal Pulp/Smoking Lung).

Crozier: "The Apocrypha of Light," "What Adam Meant When He Named It *Grass*," and "The Origin of the Species" published in *Canadian Forum*; "The Fall of Eve" published in *Atlantis*.

Rodning: "The Secret Garden" published in the *Antigonish Review*.

Sinclair: "Sestina" and "She Dreams Her Sister" published in *Event*; "All the Dreaming" published in *Grain*.

Young: "Camp-out" and "Fallen Angel" published in *Grain*.

PHOTO CREDITS

Bowering: Tony Bounsall Photo/Design
Colebrook Peace: Terry Peace
Cran: Mandelbrot
Crozier: Susan Musgrave
Heathcote: Patrick Dunae
Hunter: Glenn Hunter
Lagah: Piara Lagah
Musgrave: Barbara Pedrick
Neufeld: Black Knight Photo
Rodning: Nate Rodning
Rogers: Barbara Pedrick
Wabegijig: Leanne Flett-Kruger
Young: Clea Young

CONTENTS

PREFACE

When Diane Morriss called to tell me she wanted to title this collaboration between established poets and new voices *Breaking the Surface*, I immediately thought of Margaret Atwood's *Surfacing*, her female protagonist moving between land and water, reading the ancestral language of petroglyphs; and, of course, whales coming up for air. We are all evolving mammals and, like the humpback whales, our songs change and remain the same as we move from season to season, element to element. This book is about surprises, the sound and taste of the familiar repeating itself in fresh permutations.

I was also reminded of crème brûlée, the pleasure of seeing it on the menu, the request, the anticipation, and, best of all, the moment the spoon breaks through the thinnest crust of burnt caramel to the creamy yolks in the custard. We move through eggs, their fragile shells and golden food, to sunrises, great yolks slipping out of the horizon, and the surface tension of water, broken by waves and swimmers brave enough to re-enter the familiar element where every living thing has the option of sinking or swimming.

It is all about beginnings, the fresh smell of a baby's head, breaking the sound barrier, possibly the first thing one of the poets in this book heard on the day of her birth, if it wasn't the sound of Roger Bannister's bursting chest breaking the tape at the finish line for the four-minute mile.

As long as we live and breathe, and even afterward, we move through portals. A Spirit Dancer enters the room backwards. A Chinese baby is passed through the centre of a round loaf of bread when he or she is welcomed to the family. The family is amorphous, an organic unit that shape-shifts as family members enter and leave through the doors that define our existence.

Over the doors are the words we inscribe to mark our transitions: aubades, elegies, epithalamia, a liturgy for every human event. Like the evolving family of man and woman, the words change to fit the proper moment in history.

This year we find ourselves on a real threshold, at the beginning of a new century and a new millennium, wondering how our language will evolve to fit the brave new world. Everything is the same. In the words of Dylan Thomas, we are born, we copulate, we die. Everything is different. We have experienced Gutenberg and McLuhan, Voltaire's Bastards, the thin grey line of computer printouts. It is a time for Shelley's unacknowledged legislators of mankind to write the future of poetry, which, like life itself, changes and stays in every moment.

One of the pleasures of being a parent is watching the dialectic of the family as maturity follows the stages of nurture and rebellion. Poets are also a family and the discourse is like the dinner table with all the voices making a sometimes dissident choir. The pleasure of being a mature poet is seeing the pattern and listening for the sounds of new surfaces breaking as the chicks break through the eggs and later dive into the pond looking for those epiphanies that illuminate our private and spiritual moments.

Sono Nis Press had the idea of presenting a millennium anthology with five women poets, mature voices in the amazingly varied and rich Canadian poetry family. Victoria is a city with perfect soil for growing roses and poems. All five live in this rich cultural environment. Marilyn Bowering, Lorna Crozier, Susan Musgrave, Patricia Young, and I are friends, grateful for the healing gift of language that should and must be passed down, just as we cherish the family linens and recipes. Not a coterie, we are individual custodians of a precious tradition. All of us are teachers passionate about poetry and its healing function in the larger politics of the planet. Just as women like Phyllis Webb, P. K. Page, and Anne Szumigalski, some of our mentors, are the grandmothers of Canadian poetry, we are among the mothers and the new poets are our children.

It was our idea to introduce some of our offspring at this auspicious time so that readers of this book might watch them breaking their respective surfaces.

As in any family, the children we present, with the same awe and nervousness any mother feels at her child's first recital, are all different. We have J. William Knowles riding his twenty-four-speed bicycle "no hands" and Danielle Lagah, daughter of the Punjab, "with a double tongue in (her) soft ear." Vera Wabegijig, daughter of the Bear Clan, walks the tightrope of her cultural imperatives with no net and amazing grace. Joelene Heathcote pushes the frontiers of an alien culture while we hold our breath. Samara Brock takes a taxi back to the future and Barbara Colebrook Peace walks across the water bridging her old and new island homes.

At the time I was first reading these vital and various poems, someone asked me if I had been imbibing a bottle of bubbles. That was a very perceptive remark. We have organized this book so that the bubbles are preserved, their surfaces broken at each fresh opening. The five mature poets reveal themselves in their own new poetry and introductions, which are the skin on the air, allowing the reader to perceive the character of the family groupings. The choices and insights are fascinating.

This book affirms my affection and admiration for the poets I know and the ones I am learning. The enigmatic and mystical Marilyn Bowering has found luminous proteges with her own idiosyncratic, risk-taking, coloratura approach to the music in language. Danielle Lagah, Susan Alene Rodning, and Joelene Heathcote all look through holes in their personal history that reveal the context and design of the present the way silences access the true intention of musical notation.

Lorna Crozier, whose introductions remind me of the fresh and candid intelligence I admire in her person and poetry, brings us the compassionate audacity of poets like Brad Cran, who has already broken surfaces with his writing and editing. Lorna's choices of Cran, who wrote "Tourist is a stupid word for yourself" describing the common condition of all who travel through this life; Aislinn Hunter, the perennial expatriate; and Suzanne Buffam, who describes the journey as "lucid confusion," focus the folk idiom that is characteristic of the emerging poets in this book. Issues of gender aside, they describe a classless society evolving on common ground. If there is a new poetry, it is based on common sense and the practical life of the garden "going on without us," in Crozier's words.

Susan Musgrave, as always propelling herself through the barriers of adversity on a missile of good humour, finds a similar energy in her discoveries, all of them mature in their vision which has been informed by their experience as outsiders. Fran Bourassa, Elsie Neufeld, and Ben Perry all illustrate the essential function of loneliness in the dialectic of poetry. Compassion and humour are the catalysts that bring them into the circle. Using the garden as metaphor, as do a surprising number of these new poets living in urban times, life is affirmed in the energy of healing plants.

The connection between poetry and witchcraft is evident in this collection, which is a book of spells. There is a sense that these poets are all looking for the language that will enable the healing process of evolution. There is neither cruelty nor artifice in these poems, which is astonishing in a world where there is so

11

much cynicism. If these poets are the avant-garde of their generation, there may yet be a peaceful conclusion to the turmoil of the twentieth century.

I was moved beyond words by the silent ministrations of the lost herd "grazing round the bed" in Marlene Grand Maitre's beautiful poem about grief. Patricia Young, who beatifies the process of loss and reconciliation in her own poems charting the songlines of the inner landscape, has chosen Grand Maitre, Samara Brock, and Kathy Sinclair for their luminous storytelling.

Even when testosterone makes itself evident in the tender and muscular poems of the minority of men in this book, we are compelled toward a state of grace. That is what I found in the poems of J. William Knowles to complement my choice of Vera Wabegijig and Barbara Colebrook Peace. We are all part of the same story and, in the thoughtful words of Kathy Sinclair that bring this book to its conclusion, "Things won't ever be this way again."

There isn't a single poem here that fails to break the surface of something relevant to the millennium reader. In addition to fine poetry, this book offers a map of the relationships between past and future, mentor and mentee. I am reminded of the songlines taught to young Aboriginals, who, on reaching a certain age, are sent on a journey with the family song. That song is a map which brings the singer home. Even though the young traveller goes into the unknown, it is known, identified by the song of his antecedents—here a certain tree or a bird with a broken song.

Like all folk songs or poetry, our lyrics are mutable, but have their matrix in the great traditions of the tribe. The words change as the landscape shifts through its various seasons, but the tune belongs to the family, every permutation of which we experience through poetry. In this book, we get to be poems breaking the surface, gasping for air, like the song-changing humpback, and

12

like anglers fishing for poems big enough to keep.

Poets are a tribe to which I am proud to belong. We take what is given to us and make something beautiful for God and future generations. What could be more satisfying than that? We all hope that our pleasure will be yours and that this book will break some surfaces, creating, in the words of Leonard Cohen, "cracks the light comes through."

Out in the desert now, beyond the last chance
to buy gas or water, where songlines
were long ago invented by dreamers,
the young aboriginal is singing the song
his grandfather learned in his walkabout,
sunrise and sunset, purple and gold,
cactus with prickles and milk, frilled lizards
and kookaburra hunting for insects.

There is no way this boy who knows the words
to his grandfather's song can ever
be lost, so long as the family remembers
to bury his mother in the place where she stood
waving goodbye the morning he left.

(from "Dream Pictures of Lost")

— Linda Rogers

marilyn
bowering

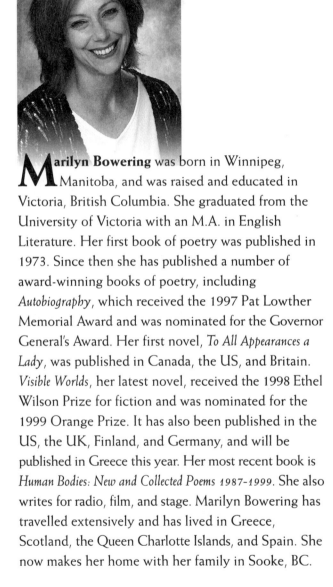

Marilyn **Bowering** was born in Winnipeg,
Manitoba, and was raised and educated in
Victoria, British Columbia. She graduated from the
University of Victoria with an M.A. in English
Literature. Her first book of poetry was published in
1973. Since then she has published a number of
award-winning books of poetry, including
Autobiography, which received the 1997 Pat Lowther
Memorial Award and was nominated for the Governor
General's Award. Her first novel, *To All Appearances a
Lady*, was published in Canada, the US, and Britain.
Visible Worlds, her latest novel, received the 1998 Ethel
Wilson Prize for fiction and was nominated for the
1999 Orange Prize. It has also been published in the
US, the UK, Finland, and Germany, and will be
published in Greece this year. Her most recent book is
Human Bodies: New and Collected Poems 1987-1999. She also
writes for radio, film, and stage. Marilyn Bowering has
travelled extensively and has lived in Greece,
Scotland, the Queen Charlotte Islands, and Spain. She
now makes her home with her family in Sooke, BC.

February

February is for coats—second-hand coats.
In the seams of your blue tailored raincoat
I've sewn animal tails.

I put on the coat and go for a walk.
Branches fly past, the great trees toss their heads.
The earth is cold, the fire banked low.
When the storm comes—later, at night—
we stop in the midst of cutting meat.

But somewhere, inside a cave,
is a wall-painting of a horse.
There are also paintings of bison,
small deer and dogs.
The colours are gold, red, ochre.
I am in the cave, painting, looking out at you
looking in at me.
I am also sewing a warm coat.

In the wind, while outside in your coat,
I met a ghost who had killed herself.
Her husband had murdered her lover;
she threw her children down a waterfall
near Tahsis.

She is distraught still.
I gave her the coat.
I came home wet.

There is no end, in February,
to pain, once it starts,

but you can ask the wind to stop.

April

April opens with a fox-brush
of snow: my house, the trees
at the back, the fall of land
to the lake turn white,
then the last of the lake-ice rots.

When we see where we are,
we're flooded: water to the back steps
and inside over the floor.
Mr. Chalker appears in gumboots
and with buckets: we sweep water
(a useless task) away from coal sacks,
suitcases, carpets, books.

I go to bed (the window blank with
melting ice), hold your sweater
to my face, and dream you are coal dust,
worms, earth.

Somewhere, not many miles from here,
is a house. If I could find it
the links of time would join.
Our room is there, the brass bedstead,
apples in the cellar,
our children and a grandmother:

my grandfather whips the little horse,
Forest, pulling the cutter:
we are cut off by the last
of spring snow:

only he can hold us in his arms,
free us to walk the hillsides,
lie in warm grass together
in summer.

When I walked to school,
long ago, I passed a wood
I called "Sad Crimes."
One time I stopped and went in:
there were broken branches shifting,
a slant light of sun or rain,
the thought-stopping musk of cedar
and moss, grey dulse tendrils
of Indian pipe underfoot:
so it was spring.

Cool white petals
swam the air: I was on a quest,
like Percival who did not have
a question to ask,

and thus I stayed silent,
behind a tree, while a man
took a shovel to wet humus,
tilled out a shining coil of worms.

Tonight I stand at the window,
there are young buds on the maple,
but I see snow from that last storm
in St. John's when I stood,
with Mr. Chalker, broom in hand,
sweeping water
like a woman.

September

1.
My friends die in September.
They talk of grammatical structures,
and then they begin to sew new clothes.

There are two sides to a pause:
you would think they would remember—
like sunlight on water   or an empty house.

I dream I'm hanging from a porthole:
when the ship veers
I am flung out—
if I can't hold on, I will die.

Those who *have* died find new life.
Their eyes touch my hands
but they have no strength.
They don't know about the ship turning sharply,
they don't know about open portholes.
I am on one side of a caesura:
my feet are wet,   I am so tired.

You would think they would recall
that all lost causes
end in September.

2.

The last time I saw you
my fingers travelled a ledge
in the dark of your room,
touched a woman's earring.

It was filigreed like a leaf,
made a sound like the sea as I brushed it.
She had breathed your breath,
misted the view, into the yard,
of late vegetables.

I was glad it was over.

I remembered my father
sawing boards in his workshop.
I recalled the faithfulness of the bee
all summer: the hive,
the honey,

the last bee dance
on the windowsill.

December

In December, "every form that you see
has its original in the Divine world."
Death is of no consequence,
because there is still eternity.

But I am grieved.
I bend my head to drink from the rivulet
of limitless waters. People step in and out
of it. Timeless water drips from
my lips. It is no substitute for the words
of a friend;

it does not remember intelligence or faith,
it cannot recall to me—you who have finished
with this world—what it meant to have been
with you in a wood at night—

some small light,
or small animal saved.
Who can forget

a moment like a match struck
on the teeth of a zipper?
I hoard it
for the long winter.

Pass into that mighty deep, if you must,
so that the one drop which is yourself
may become a sea:

but do not drown.
Put on your shoes,
set out as if to visit me:

we came into the world;
we knew we would have to leave it.

joelene Heathcote

J **oelene Heathcote** was born in Nanaimo, British Columbia, in 1975, and has lived in various small towns between Qualicum Beach and Victoria. In 1996, she moved to Seoul, South Korea, to write and to teach English. This experience became the grist for a collection of poems titled "Skins for a New Identity." She is currently working on a novel titled "Hunger on the Thirty-Eighth Parallel." In the last year she has published poetry, reviews, and creative non-fiction in various magazines and newspapers including the *Antigonish Review,* the *Globe and Mail,* and *Event.* She received a B.A. in English and Creative Writing from Malaspina University College in 1999, and is planning to continue on to a graduate degree in English.

SKINS FOR A NEW IDENTITY

"The reason I keep going back to poetry," says Joelene Heathcote, "is because the version of truth I'm looking for still hasn't emerged and like an archaeologist I'm drawn back to the digging site." Joelene's site is the soft ground between a man and a woman, between cultures, and on the treacherous ground of moral ambiguity. It is also, I suggest, a life's work.

One of the first tests for a poet of talent is to step away from what she already knows to cross the threshold and venture into the unknown—away from friends and family and those who support her vocation as a poet—in order to assess the reach of her gift: to risk the truth she knows for what she might yet find. Joelene Heathcote's motivation in going to Korea was to live close to the marrow. Having spent her life to that point as part of the majority in her home culture, she wanted to examine what it was like to be an outsider, a stereotype for others, and to make herself vulnerable; to learn what it feels like to be "naked" (without the protection of language), and by doing so piece together what and where she had come from. I've often thought that this combination of courage and curiosity is what marks out the poet who will continue to grow from those who, having found a species of certainty, fall away. When there doesn't appear to be a line separating life and poetry—when life *is* poetry and the search for truth inside both is what drives her—not only are you looking at a poet who won't remain comfortably within given boundaries, but you are seeing one who won't let you, the reader, remain comfortably within your boundaries either.

This is the political and social poetry of the heart, a stripping away of race, gender, size, and language to find not the cliché of a meeting place, but a limit. As I have grown to know Joelene (having been introduced to her poetry gently, persistently, by one of her former teachers, the poet Kevin Roberts), I've found myself thinking about her remark to me early on that "innocence and vulnerability are connected." These are principal qualities of her poems—the appealing openness they have—and they also go hand in hand with the development of wisdom. To read these poems is to step into that vulnerability and emerge a little raw and more finely tuned.

Your Own Brother

And Jesus saw Nathanael and he said, "Here is a real Israelite;
there is nothing false in him!" — John 1:47

Light nor air is allowed
in this room with its windows papered shut.
Nathanael, brother. Twenty-one when blood
permeates his eyes, his pupils dilating
to become solitary satellites.

Seven days of waiting and he mumbles
faintly from a cistern of memory trailers—asks,
"What have they done to me?" in the drawn-out sigh
of a tire losing air, morphine like a cold snake
through the swollen parts of his brain.
He does not mean the doctors
who ask the impossible questions of his name and the date
or the loud nurses who keep him dull with needles. No,
when he says *they*, he means the pack of youths
whose locked limbs made a ring of flesh
he could not escape, their mouths swearing death.
He is referring to the invisible boy
emerging from the impure dark
to deal him six blows to the skull with a bat
before he fell hard against his own driveway
bleeding from his ears, mind ringing.

Go ahead, bend down to stroke the heavy wool of dark curls,
press your lips to the sweating brow that smells of maple syrup.
You can do nothing. Hold him
when the bathroom mirror shows him

what they have done to his face
and later when you see what is done to his soul.
His anger is not with you, his only sibling.
It's because he can no longer hear. Is lost.
Feel him push you away,
not because you leave, close the door like a verdict
and are free, but because he is captive
and when he closes his stinging eyes
against your unfamiliar face,
the only place he goes, is in.

Megook Saram

Driving past the telephone box
outside a *Sangey* grocer, he is dizzy
at the sight of pig tails,
my vermilion summer dress
like a flag for the bull.
I turn and our eyes meet, his mouth hissing
pabo megook saram. Stupid American.

Into the phone I say, *I am no longer me.*

He has seen me before, on the internet
site, bookmarked *megook*.
A weapon to dissect sex. Now
I'm the white girl looking out,
instead of him peering in.

When he pulls up in front,
he recognizes the bare skin of my thighs
but I have fewer pixilations.
He knows me, but my face and hair lack
the rose glow belonging to Russian prostitutes
beneath warming lights in *Chongno Samga*.
He has seen me in films, in advertisements for
Buffalo jeans, sprawled naked in *Playboy*.
My true nationality—multi-median.

He leans over the passenger seat
rolls down the window, smiles.
I indicate five minutes.
And he unzips his fly in the cool comfort

of leather Hyundai interior.
His smooth business hand working
himself to maddening explosion
with thoughts of young tanned breasts.
I am speechless, his precedence set:
voice does nothing without translation.

When I turn back toward him,
replace the phone in the cradle
he is reaching for a box
of soft Kleenex on the dash,
his face and hands glistening,
body vibrating with American sex—
looking through me,
because he has seen me.

For him, I am *megook*—American
imperialist. Canada doesn't matter.
I am white, empty   continental.
No longer me.
Down load.

Silpun Sarang

(Sangey Dong, Seoul)

Waking in the August dawn
of an alien city, you prop yourself up
on your elbow to watch your wife's eyes
travel blindly behind their closed lids,
the thin bones of her lashes
fluttering like wings of tethered moths.

You fold back the bed sheet,
run your hand along the heaving summit
of her white breasts—a path in your memory
that leaves your throat tight.
        Beside you in this humid room
she is spread-eagled and dreaming of flight.

Although you do not see her mouth
moving beneath the grey silk
of a Korean morning, you feel
the slow vibration of a foreign name
oscillating in the static air.

Below the window the city blooms
in the sepia glow of metropolitan sunrise.
        An Asian man rides past on his bicycle.
The loud squeak of his ill-working brakes, a *déjà vu*
that has beckoned you from bed,
a sound so shrill you feel it in your mouth,
could swear he was in the room.

You have to see his face
to know the content
of your wife's dreams.
So you watch him approaching,
try the name she's uttered.
And his puzzled gaze is on you, twisting
your frantic mind everywhere—
back to the body of your wife,
on to the *fait accompli*.

You close your eyes, pray silently
for the screech of an automobile,
the crunch of metal into metal,
      the faithless scream of the cyclist
head crumpling back into heart.

Seoul wobbles on the surface of your eyes.
      The cyclist escapes down a narrow street
zephyr rolling in his ears, chest heaving
for *you* he'd never seen
but your woman he knew by heart.

You shout his name again
and it falls, dissolving in rush hour traffic
and the blades of a passing helicopter
beating the air in time
with your mind.

And Suddenly She Is Gone

At the edge of the Han River
they sit silently. Neither their hands,
nor any part of them is touching.
But they are in love.
Or one of them is. She picks her fingernail,
considers briefly before trading him this poem
for a paper cup of honey tea.
It's foreign trade for them, simple business:
her language for his love.

> *His wife will be home.*
> *The cool light of April fading*
> *through the halls of the narrow apartment.*

She begins to wonder how they got here—
how the months passed
in the sigh of traffic, wave folding over wave,
she folding over him.

> *The next morning, his wife*
> *washes his shirt, her bitten fingers*
> *find this poem—a Canadian heart*
> *transcribed.*

Everything has its price.
The day of her departure, they say little.
It was always that way. He takes her hand,
pushes his way through the crowded airport.
Canada is an impossible green space
on the other side of the globe.

Time is a hammer on their hearts.
It's the way these things go, she says, but she's not sure.
He doesn't hear her, checks his watch
against the flight board. She thinks
about involuntary operations and dealings.
What is the cost of their union?

Her paper cup, sweet tea gone,
drifts on the banks of the Han River.

Jung Chun Hea

(Sangey Dong, Seoul)

In Seoul, at night
there is nothing
but the guttural growl
of a city at near rest
and the weeping
of my Korean friend
on a long leash to China.

She whispers to the receiver
that she misses his love,
traces his name in English
on her foot, circles it
in pen until she draws blood.
So much water between them—
what good are feet anyway?

The man on the telephone
is her husband, three years absent
on *business*—in Hong Kong he lies
half-in, half-out of a dream,
one hand jammed in the dark
warm space of a concubine's thighs,
the other cupped loosely under her left breast—
the phone slipping slowly
from between his shoulder and ear.

Chun Hea has never been to China, but it exists
in her mind as a place of wet alleys,
clotheslines of tiny flickering lamps,

a country where romance eddies
like flaming paper boats.

Here, it is customary to wait.
        I go out to the verandah,
flick my cigarette off the edge,
watch it drift and fall
and drift.

Tonight on the fourth floor
of what feels like outer space,
women sit alone in adjacent apartments,
flickering in the purple heart beats
of their television sets, and everywhere
the hum of the butterfly
is deafening.

danielle lagah

Danielle Lagah was born in 1977 in Victoria, British Columbia. In addition to poetry, she writes short fiction and screenplays, and is currently working on a novel. Lagah is a third-year student at Malaspina University College in Nanaimo, where she studies writing, political science, and languages.

These poems are part of a series dealing with the history of Danielle's family, and the cultural separations that arise between generations. Of the series, she says: "For my own part in it, it's coming to terms with what it means to be a half-breed, what it means to live in limbo, with Punjabi in your blood but not in your mouth. But mostly I'm trying to explore the world of my family—and the idea of family in general." She hopes to one day publish the entire series in book form.

CONSTRUCTING FAMILY

I met Danielle Lagah in a workshop I was teaching at Malaspina University College. What struck me at once about her poems was her ability to get inside character, to make the empathic link that is the secret of all linkages a writer makes to reach out into the world. The ability to feel as if you are another in order to understand his or her experience, to present that view of the world with emotional authority, and also to convey insight into your own, is more commonly a hard-won reward for years of following the poetic path. Danielle Lagah seems to have grasped it at once: mastering, in a remarkably short space of time, all the craft required to articulate the texture of feeling and story surrounding her family.

What is also notable is that the "I"—the observer who, Danielle has remarked in speaking of these poems, was "at a loss as to how to connect [with her heritage] because of cultural differences," takes no false steps. We believe her "reportage" because it includes the mystery of meaning. Her images present both the inside and the outside story: the associations of individual memory, operating according to individual logic, that we apprehend at once as truth. In all cases, too, the emotional veracity of the whole (what it must feel like to be in the warp and weft of this family) takes precedence over the gesture—the surge for the dramatic you'd expect from a more showy, and shallow, poet. Danielle's poems resonate, one with the other, giving us a particular music of perspective, of voices; an interplay of grief, miracles, faith, injustice, bewilderment, anger—family.

For the first generation of a family born here (Danielle's generation), removed from the source of landscape, history, language—culture—that has "always" given the family identity, a generation hearing only the echoes of culture without knowing

it directly themselves, the response is often one of nostalgia—
sometimes, in the poet Andrei Voznesensky's phrase, a "nostalgia
for the present" as well as for the past. There's not a hint of
nostalgia here. The view is cooler, implacable in its knowledge
of what it sees and understands. It has its own procedures,
vulnerability, and pain and yet takes it all in with an unwavering
gaze.

Danielle has said that she set out to "preserve . . . things worth
writing down and sharing." Her instincts as a poet have taken
her further; how far she *can* go I don't know, but a lot of us will be
paying attention.

Glossary of Terms
mahnji—grandmother
naht—run
surma—a traditional liquid black eyeliner
bhangra—a dancing party; also a form of music
supp—snake or serpent
shaa—shadow (closest Romanized spelling to original Doabi)
pani—water
roti—bread; also the word for Indian flatbread

Note: There is some dispute as to the English spellings of these words,
given that the Punjabi language comprises several dialects. Wherever
possible I have tried to use the spelling closest to that of my father's
village, Pubwan.

Glossary of Characters (in relation to the narrator)
Piara—father
Mahnji / Swarni—grandmother
Old Mahnji Chinti—great-grandmother
Manga / Buppa—grandfather
Jeet—uncle
Piari—aunt

My Father Was in a Coma Half His Early Life

They carried him, my grandma and Ratha Siwami
on a stretcher through the Himalayas
they thought he was possessed

He remembers waking up once
in a monastery in the mountains, seeing
monks in red robes chanting in a circle
a flagpole rising by itself in the centre

They bathed him in holy water
washed the sores all over his body
spat in his mouth
years later a Canadian doctor would say it was tuberculosis

My grandma knelt down in the high woods
and planted a tree there, prayed for six days
If Piara lives, he will come back and
water this tree
she had already lost one child

Naht

Jeet (Brother):

All season we saved
the new puppies and old
sick dogs too
Piara and me, we lifted them
over the mud wall
when the police came feeding
their handfuls of sweet lardu
stuffed with poison

The village will be overrun with mange
they said, *these dogs will steal*
the bread from babies
and my auntie said it too
shaking her finger at us
from over her washing

but we lifted them
over the mud wall
felt their furred bellies
hearts beating in our hands before
we let them drop
into the wide fields of wheat
and called out *Run Run*
Run

Rattle

Swarni (Mother):

> Piari was buried and Piara's sickness came
> I saw it writhe in the soil, slide toward him
> It came from the ground, from the grave
> Like a lithe *shaa*, great *Supp*, diamond-backed
> it crept up the leg of his white funeral pants
>
> When I was a girl
> my mother wouldn't let me walk
> to school alone, past the sugar cane
> where *Supp* slept in a black coil, waiting
> to wrap himself around my legs
> stick his double tongue in my soft ear
> I wore bells on my ankles, stomped
> like a boy past the sweet green stalks and
> said my prayers
>
> When I saw Piara's sickness come
> I knew at once
> tore the bells from my ankles to shake them
> rattle the shadow from my son

For My Grandfather (I)

You went to England and
left a hole in my history
stretches of sub-continents,
immasculine time. Your face
interrupts my hot climates, mud
huts; you hang in a snowy split-screen
Southhall fashion. Blow freezing rain
into Jalandhar's red dust

You are non-essential. The Pubwan
seasons go by; drought and blood and
love. It is Mahnji who bears children, throws
dirt on their graves. She keeps
her eyes level with the seam of the land
searching for your clean winter

Years later my father went to London
and tried to piece you together

*

Piara (Son):

There's this bar in Southhall next to a laundromat—
the beer tastes like soap. I met Uncle Lal there for drinks
and I asked him about my dad, about the six missing
years, the time we guess at
when he was far away, working in London. Lal is old
(the last one alive who can tell me) he can't remember
much, and it's almost too late

Lal (Uncle):

Manga always wore a nice suit, you know, I never
saw him in poor clothes. He had his shoes custom
made in Auldgate. Once he came for dinner
and brought the girls a present each. Silver bangles

We sat across from each other at the wood table
Lal in an old tweed suit jacket
cigarette burns on the lapels, blowing smoke in my face
He ordered more beer because
I was paying
He was there that night my dad was stabbed, I asked him
to tell me what happened and he told me

> We were in a bar and Manga had just got a letter
> from your mother, I don't know what it said, but
> he was drinking and drinking
> He had a mug and it was half full of scotch, I don't
> remember what happened but there was a fight
> and he picked up a barstool

Lal leaned in, his breath like bad milk

> He hit this guy with a stool and the guy pulled a knife
> small blade and jabbed it in
> Manga stood there with the knife in his stomach
> somehow he still fought, smashed in a jaw, a nose—
> he picked the guy up

Lal told me

He threw him down the stairs. Broke
his neck. Manga pulled out
the knife himself, that's all I know

Piara (Son):

For all of my life I will write that letter in my head, the one
my dad was reading before he became a killer. Sometimes it says
Piari is dead and these are the times I love my dad
and think it was only the drink and that he was so blind with grief
he could break a man's neck
And sometimes the letter says *We're leaving for Canada*
and these are the times I hate him
and think he was mean and scared
and wanted to keep us
prisoner in the crude country of his head

For My Grandmother

You cook in an almond kitchen. Curry smells
cling to the walls, the furniture. This is the same chair
I have always sat in—white vinyl with yellow flowers;
the same banana and apple in a wicker bowl. Bells
on your ankles flash as you bend
scoop flour with a tin cup

Your life has been a bending down
Your muscles move comfortably that way
humbled. Picking wheat, onions
lifting babies, your face
to the man you married

How do you cook like that, weed
the gardens in those yards of patterned
silk? Gold chains, bracelets, bells. How
can you bend so low
and not topple?

                    Your body is the dam
                    in the river; you
brace
                    yourself, hands buried
in a muddy bank
                    eyes squeezed tight
Stopping
                    the flood of progress
        My Mahnji

What was it like to lose a child?
Your oldest daughter poisoned, asleep
in a green death. How did you grieve?
The rest of your babies have grown
and married this country, taught
their own daughters to do the same
Are we weak to you? Canadian
women climbing the hills of industry
embracing our isolation

Flour (III)

Swarni:

Once, when Piara was sick
there was a drought
and the wheat didn't grow

The fields, miles of straw stocks and yellow dirt
grains swirling in the wind, buffalo crying

He would eat nothing but roti
and there was no wheat

Birds peck. The boy's white bed soaked in sweat
his back a wellspring
open sores blooming in the heat, red yellow black

I pulled my sleeves up;
went to the fields with a bowl

Sun-dust in his throat, stomach crying for bread
his mother's red scarf outside, blowing around her
framed in the window

I plucked single grains
one by one from the ground

Bare feet, back arched, bones knotting
silk sticking, sweat
on her thighs, forehead. Fingers sifting through
dirt, searching

After a long time I filled the bowl
I crushed the wheat and made flour

The boy coughing in the bed; *pani*

Enough for one roti

pounding will and son-love in to the dough

I lit the oven, cooked it

the boy on his back, breathing bread smells
opens his eyes

I looked up and saw the crow
descending

The Trees in That Country

All you taught me were numbers
Count to ten,
I can still do it

Show me a tree. In English: green
brown, tuber, trunk, rind, stump
leaf, flower
fruit on the bough, fruit on the ground
I picture Okanagan apple orchards
Nanoose Arbutus. West Coast Spruce and Oak
Show me a tree, dad

You struggle, your mouth shifting to that
other language. Those soft *j*'s and hard *ee*'s
n's that don't exist on the page. I know
there are words for trees in this tongue, words
that say things I can never understand
foreign pictures

In my head a Douglas Fir
grows in the centre of a Jalandhar field, its footing
in sugar cane soil. I am

tired of language, of my trapped tongue
in its crude patterns. Why give me
those ten numbers? Tiny things
for the wide inner spaces I saved, ten needles
on an empty pine tree—
were these all
you could spare?

For My Great-Grandmother

Old Mahnji Chinti, always seemly
your tattoos
were a childhood riddle
Deep blue ink absorbed
by your tissue skin, the pictures
long ago feathered with age
The first time I saw them
I was eight, kneeling on the kitchen stool
elbows on the gold-flecked melamine
of your sink counter. You pushed
up the white sleeves of your cardigan
and I glimpsed the strange dye
before your arms were plunged
into dish soap bubbles. For years after
I waited for you to push up your sleeves

At eleven I had a vision
you as a girl
standing in an Indian temple
held down by priests
who drew symbols of your new womanhood
with cobalt needles and chanted
in Hindi, your
eyes squeezed tight and tears
greyed by *surma* staining
your gold-thread sari

When I was sixteen
I watched at Pargan's bhangra
while you danced

bare arms over your head
the blue ink peeking out
from between bouncing bangles
in the dance floor light
hands twisting like swan heads

Two years later
I had enough courage
a grown woman, finally
to ask
while you lay in the hospital
healing from a broken rib
I touched them
your blue tattoos
and I asked

I was a young woman, you said
and every dry season in Jasomajara
the carnival would come
I went with my best girls and we all
got tattoos

the man that did mine was handsome
and I giggled so my arms shook
while he worked
I was always punished after—
my mother would smack my face
But every dry season
I would go again
and get another

You smiled an unseemly smile
and ran your skinny finger over
each cerulean story

This is a flower
This is a peacock
This is my name

Susan **Alene Rodning** was born in Prosser, Washington, and finished high school in California, where she also took her first singing lessons. She came to Canada when she was twenty-one. She has been employed as a nurse and a medical social worker, and is now working privately on solutions to problems of violence and sickness. Her first poem, "The Child," was written at Fort San, Saskatchewan, at a poetry workshop. Previously she had written a story as part of a correspondence course—that story was "Town Pump," and it won the Saskatchewan Writers' Guild Prize; her second story, "Marathon," won too. Each prize included time at Fort San, studying writing. She seemed to step from one genre to another until she had poetry tracks in her non-fiction, and "ping" in her poetry. ("Ping," of course, belongs to singing.) It was only when she looked back on the journey that she saw that purpose is what unites the otherwise imprecise language of words.

A CLEARING IN THE WOODS

Not always, not even very often, does a poet present us with the gift of an inner landscape so thoroughly inhabited that it reaches us at the level of our own inner world, inviting correspondences, making a meeting place, or a circle of "felt" knowledge that exists outside of time. Such poems take us instantly into the world of dream and myth and to the roots of poetry: the journey over the threshold into the unknown, and back; the primacy of naming the elemental world; the order and power of song. This is Susan Alene Rodning's gift. Her poems stand where the boundary between worlds is thin, gaze both ways, and bring art, knowledge, and experience to the vision.

I initially encountered Rodning not as a poet but as the mysterious "opera singer" who could be heard from the beach at Hutchison Cove, near where I live. Her voice—which may be leading her into a musical career—is big, resonant with experience, and not out of place, scale, or tone with the rocks, cedars, sea, ducks, swans, osprey, seals—the centred peace of the cove. Our meeting in person was accidental. She had heard me speak at a memorial for the late poet Robin Skelton, and since Robin had taken an interest in her work, editing a selection of poems for a pamphlet (*Unwritten Letters*) published for the Hawthorne Society by Reference West, she thought I might know where and how she could connect with other poets since coming to live "in the woods." It was a surprise to both of us to find we were neighbours.

Like all the best poetry, explaining the magic of Susan Alene Rodning's work is difficult—like cupping water in the hands. In her poems, the sure voice standing at a still point to tell us about time and timelessness shape-shifts. It is the drowsy child who finds herself by finding herself in other living creatures, and who can lead us through the world "written on our palms" that Rodning so carefully articulates. It is both creator and subject looking to the work both have made, to understand what they are; it plays between subject and object, inner and outer, blurring distinctions between the self and other and God. Like the picture on the Ajax can, each vision exists inside another: the self haunts the self and is both itself and a ghost; it watches the dream and the dreamer and what the dream sees.

These are not only the mysteries of perception, but of being. They are also the story of a journey, looking under the skin of things: the journey of aloneness that the poet who has dared to step across the threshold into light and shadow is obliged to make.

The Luminous Tree

I stood in the landscape of the fantasy you painted;
over your shoulder I saw the open door,
the night in twilight
and the luminous tree that arched and bent,
a free-standing monument of creation.
Each limb, my many hands called and stroked
in the voice of years, it thrust itself out of earth
into heaven.

You stroked my eyes with lips, as with your brush,
made a sensuous dream of ordinary lines;
now a stern mother who will reproach,
and then a child in your arms reaching up
into the eyes of the man in every way a child.
You too look to the portrait for meaning
and see the mesh of one who plays babbling sounds
that can't be deciphered.
Each shining branch a glimpse of the one who holds,
the web of a hand as hollow as his arms.
I turn from silence to roots driven like spikes to anchor me,
yet wind will carry him away.
He fondles my breast for the word
that will fill his loneliness.
Though I kiss for a moment the lines of his years,
I myself age. There are no lines written,
only the sound of a door in an empty room.
The tree reaches to clutch my wanderlings;
the direction of my will gropes like a seedling.

It was a strange time
when I spoke from the landscape of his fantasy.
Walking as I heard and grieved,
now as the child, then as the crazy old woman.
But I was never so insane
as when the words spoke without me.

A Himalayan

He said it was a Himalayan cat
that I needed to bring me back.
What does he know about anger
I can't tell? I watch
for a solution
on the small black and white TV.

Colour, he said, will bring it faster.
I thought he meant cats
but then he spoke of stations, times,
and I saw the Himalayan fold into himself
until he was only hair.
Now I'm hoping for an answer in a colour TV.

Lying on my couch I can be swayed,
cry for the woman who lost her man
in a fight over something about a baby.
And in-laws are at it again.
Lost in another woman's story,
I cuddle into a ball,
roll over once and switch stations
to watch a lover's quarrel as the Himalayan
curls at my feet.

He said I needed colour,
but rage marks red into me no matter what the words.
And crying comes in blue sounds.
Don't be afraid, the grey cat says,
walking circles round my reasons
for wanting out.

I made a fence to hold the cat but
forgot to colour a passage
that would let me out.
I sit within my borders, the Himalayan outside,
watching fear dance.

Pausing to see more clearly,
I catch a glimpse of what remains:
the food on the plate is spoiled,
the water stagnant.

The scene is black and white:
settling in the small square room
the TV speaks to me in predictable scenarios.
Still I wonder how it will turn out.

The Wandering Eyes of the Dream

In the telling, I see you as I am,
hands open on a dry plain,
feeling a drop in the palm.
I have no name for the emotion
as thoughts tumble over words.
You are the cry I heard in me
before the tree fell at your door.
I find a fire in the hearth;
closing the door, I'm home.
Who welcomes me here?
I am an unexpected ghost
disturbing a restful sleep.
In your corner, I hover
and watch the eyes of the dream open
onto another clearing.

The Secret Garden

1.

She cried and slept throughout the events;
now vines twist branches over the garden.
She ate fruit and biscuits;
being thirsty, she drank; drowsy, she slept.
Waking, she listened for the house of silence,
counting a hundred rooms in bone;
opened doors will close,
to be found the remembered day.

Red-breasted bird, sing a winter song,
burst my walls.

2.

I am the child
looking from an unmirrored room
closed by those who mourn.
>   *I seek darkness*
>   *and know it cannot hide me,*
>   *I beg again: child, child,*
>   *be hidden from me.*

I creep down my narrow halls
hearing groans in the rooms, in my bones;
I step again
to unleash the victim.

3.

The gate is high;
with a toehold in the ironwork

she boosts herself up,
peeks into the keyhole.
She sees a garden,
pears and apples upon vines,
a path cobbled in porcelain,
a gabled house with ivy walls,
gold-trimmed windows.

The old bearded man only she can see
gazes at her from his window.

4.
Her garden her nest,
she is the missal-thrush
in rooms of stone.
The secret, stranger than many rooms
or than the garden?

Taking the candle to the corridor
she opened to the Someone who cried.

> Boychild, silent night waiting for the bright moon,
> calling me, ghost who has spoken: touch the edge.
> Dreams of seeing are not real.
> In the hidden-away room, dream of the garden
> locked in your years.

Spring, sun on rain,
mends the growing limb.
A thorn bores into flesh.
Earth must be loosed.

5.

Rain forced the seed
earthed in sod.
Flying from a wall,
red-breasted bird:
you mustn't stir
silence in the grass.
He is building a nest;
pretend not to see.
Be a bird,
settle in your waiting nest.
Whistle low,
speak to flying wing:
I'm wild myself, the child sang,
flying into a corner of the bright eye.

6.

Draw your breath, traveller.
A son cries somewhere: *Father, Father.*
He walked 'til moonrise hearing the cry;
thinking it a dream, he slept, seeing
the clear spring burst open the garden.

Children led him
into the wilderness he planted,
gentled earth his prize.

Invasions

Summers and winters joined,
roads blocked by snow in winter,
floods in summer. Father remembered
making his way to his Dakota home to hear of invasion,
Hitler in Norway. All he could see was his mother,
sixteenth child of sixteen.
Her mother died with her birth,
her only task to multiply the land
that few would live to see.
Who is left now to see land, cleared and cherished,
invaded? The narrow fjord lies
beneath mountain fortresses.

You cleared the land you never owned.
The goat-herd, seeing the grass grow long upon his roof,
sent the goat to feed; now there is no growth.
The *starbonde* takes the yield to himself;
his wealth is wisdom with none to share;
you belong to him like the trees you've cleared.

Step down into your dirt-floored house.
The crossbeams protect you; the howl is passed in *skoling*.
The floor is dirt, a cold only noticed
as spirit leaves the fjord and mountains.

Bergit left that Norwegian home as a child
wearing the bone of her ancestors who searched
the clearing place. She came to America,
called it Land of Toil, wore the bone before me,
searching for a place to clear.

Syver claimed only land enough to stand.

Tongues fail, the plough scatters;
pride, kept silent,
burst the anguish of children.

Always in the dreaming night,
the fog deepened and the train came,
passing over the land of Syver's bones.
Land is lost in passing.

Grief beat, drums on bone.
Bergit died in my bone wearing.
The vision, clear in the blind,
is blurred for me now.
In the clearing
earth invades my vision.

Untitled

Your roaring makes a listener
of me. I go along your shores,
tides high, wind dashing your waters
on rocky cliffs. I listen for the sound
of molluscs in the sand.

Wet footprints mark the journey;
I see how I follow.
Lifting the skin of sea,
I find the many-chambered nautilus,
the landscape of reason
that walks on alone.

Within These Walls

In my house I live alone.
I'm child and mother to the child;
waking, I attend to the helpless one
who slept in me.

By evening the child becomes
the older one who comes late
to find rest.

Evening lights a candle on my table;
now I'm mother, spreading my plenty before you.
I'm the empty one. The child whimpers
to suck at my breast, her cry, a wanting sound.
Needing a home.

I'm the old woman hoping to walk away.
Limbs are fixed by crooked dreams
that lead me into darkness,
spoken in a language I never heard.

Immigrant longing for a childhood home,
I run into the mother's land
wanting to be filled.
Land is whole
at the feet of the mother.

Lorna
Crozier

Lorna Crozier's *Inventing the Hawk* received the Governor General's Award for Poetry in 1992, the Pat Lowther Memorial Award for the best book of poetry by a Canadian woman, and the Canadian Authors' Association Award for poetry. *Everything Arrives at the Light* received the 1995 Pat Lowther Award, and a selection of poems from that book was awarded the *National Magazine* Gold Medal. Two of her other books were nominated for the Governor General's Award, and a series of her poems won the CBC competition in 1984. Her tenth book of poetry, *What the Living Won't Let Go*, was published by McClelland and Stewart in the spring of 1999. Her poems have been translated into several languages, and she has read her work across Canada and in such countries as South Africa, Chile, Malaysia, France, Italy, and England. Her latest publication is a collection she edited called *Desire in Seven Voices*, essays on desire by Canadian women writers. Lorna Crozier presently teaches in the Department of Writing at the University of Victoria and lives in Saanichton, British Columbia, with poet Patrick Lane.

The Apocrypha of Light

On the first day, light said
Let there be God and there was God—
light needed a shape to move inside,
a likeness thick-maned and tawny. It strode
into the absence we call night
and what it touched and tongued
sparked visible then glowed, warmed by
its golden spittle.

It splashed and rolled in water
till rivers and seas could not be parted
from its gleam.
                    It lingered: on the hourglass
of August pears, on blackbird, bear scat,
calves' blood, on the hand of the beloved,
its unlikely flare.

It slipped into the darkest corners
then suddenly it stumbled—
stopped—
hid its brightness and would not move.

What in the dark did it wish it hadn't seen?
What in the dark of rancour and despair,
sorrow glimpsed once and never passing?
What after that could bring it back
to all that waited for its sheen:

arbutus limbs, an otter's head
just above the sea, orange pips, zinfandel,
a panther's muscled plush.

Now you make a list of things.
Remember light's likeness, remember too
this is the beginning of the first day.

The Origin of the Species

. . . but the old man only said that it was pointless
to speak of there being no horses in the world for
God would not permit such a thing.

—Cormac McCarthy, *All the Pretty Horses*

Drenched with dawn
eohippus, smaller than a fox,
walked out of chaos.

She struck the sand. Water
gushed from her hoofprint,
drops flying through the air

and where they fell
the sky came down to rest
and a thousand miracles of grass

meadowed the desert.
For centuries eohippus lived
satisfied and self-contained

then her legs and muzzle lengthened,
muscles pushed against
her withers, thickened her neck.

Now ready for the wind
she made it lean and boneless,
its mane and tail visible

across the sky. Imagine horse
and wind running in the sun's
warm pastures before the fall

before blackfly, horsefly,
heartworm, rider. Imagine
the two of them alone

an appaloosa, maybe, and a grey
adrift in the absolute
beatitude of grass,

no insect buzzing,
no rope or bridle.
In the mornings of that lost

and long ago beginning,
nothing broken
or in need of breaking.

A Lesson in Perspective

A cat creates the world
with a paw's touch, with a stroke of his whiskers,
intricate parallel drawings like a lesson in perspective
where no lines meet.

The colours are a cat's colours,
the many greys and sepias of shade,
light's glossolalia on a blade of grass
quivering in the slightest breeze.

After warbler and nuthatch,
after thrush, chickadee and finch,
the cat makes mouse, bumblebee and spider,
then the small blue butterfly that beats
on the rilled roof of his mouth,
a word with wings.

The cat makes words with fangs, too,
with hooves, fins and tusks. He sees
a word that moves so lightly across the mind
it must be a grey nectar-sipping moth,
feet of such small and delicate design
they walk on petals and leave no bruise.

The Fall of Eve

When the animals used to talk to me—
lisp of snail, click of grasshopper's
exact consonants, dolphin's diphthong
slipping through the waves—there were rumours
a woman, perhaps with wings, roamed
the wasteland. They said she was furred,
sleek and shimmering as a weasel, eyes
wells of clearest water where you'd surely drown.

Not knowing what she feared,
I washed the smell of man from my skin,
walked to where the garden stopped
and everything Adam couldn't name
fell into poetry and silence.

It was a place you sensed
you were watched, caught in a gaze
that made you beautiful and strange.

The serpent was the last I understood,
his voice stayed after tyger's,
after hawk's, wolf's and rat's.
When he offered me the apple
I bit because I wanted what his tongue
had licked and polished to a shine.

At the hawthorn hedge, good and evil
sweet in my mouth, I said *Lilith*
though I didn't remember
what it meant, then I said *my sister*

and something like a breath lifted
the hair on the back of my neck.

Though I couldn't see
through shadows I grasped
she is what I've lost. God's voice
roared through the leaves
and I glimpsed wings unfolding,
blue feathers bewildering the other blue of sky.

My own arms rose and I knew
the way you know your own sorrow
on this earth, once I was that dear,
that close to her, once I too could fly.

What Adam Meant When He Named It *Grass*

An infinite
and singular intelligence:
eel, hairgrass, crab,
canary, fescue, ribbon,
zebra, spear, foxtail, marsh,
papyrus, little quaking,
bluegrass, buffalo, brome,
cocksfoot, lovegrass, grama,
bulrush, horsetail, bog—
deep-rooted slender tongues
that lick the light
for salt.

Aislinn Hunter

Aislinn Hunter was born in Ontario, where she
lived until she was nineteen. She then moved
to Dublin, Ireland. When she came back to Canada,
she settled on the West Coast and began a degree in
Creative Writing and Art History at the University
of Victoria. After completing her B.F.A., she moved
to Vancouver, where she completed an M.F.A. in
Creative Writing. Over the years her work has
appeared in a number of Canadian periodicals,
including *Grain*, *Event*, the *Malahat Review*, *Prairie Fire*,
and the *Antigonish Review*, as well as in *Poetry Ireland
Review*, *Poetry New Zealand* and *Stand* (UK). In 1996
her short story "Hagiography" was nominated for the
Journey Prize. Her non-fiction has been broadcast
on CBC Radio, where she is an active freelancer
producing radio documentaries on the arts. Aislinn
Hunter recently completed her first novel, entitled
"What Remains," and she is at work on a poetry
manuscript.

SOME BEAUTIFUL THING YOU HAVE MADE

Aislinn Hunter was part of one of those wonderful workshops where you know as a teacher that at least a third of the participants have been struck by the magic wand of poetry and will go on to make their mark as writers. There were Billeh Nickerson, who writes a column for *Xtra* and who will soon have a book published by Arsenal Pulp Press; Carla Funk, whose first book came out with Coteau this fall; Rebecca Frederickson, whose poems about a northern Alberta farm have appeared in dozens of literary magazines across the country; and Aislinn, a passionate commentator on all of their work, and an assertive and articulate advocate for the best words in the best order.

All that year, or was it the next, she wrote about her homesickness for Ireland—even though she was born in small-town Ontario. At first I found her obsession puzzling, but now I think Ireland is her poetic homeland, birthplace of Yeats and more recently of Heaney, Muldoon, and Boland, to name a few. Like Gwendolyn MacEwen's Middle East, it's become an essential part of her poetic sensibility. You can hear the country's cadences and its elegiac response to history in some of her lines, especially when she reads out loud.

From the start, Aislinn never wrote small. Her poems never took the route of skinny imagist responses to the world. Instead, her affirmation that the past and the present are inextricable led her into long, almost prose-like lines and the kind of movements through time that characterize fiction. Her poems, in fact, sometimes feel like highly condensed novels. The character who speaks, and who is both her and not her, is a time traveller, one who imagines the past so well that she makes it palpably present.

The poems about her family evoke the real characters who make up her life, but they also move far beyond the literal. The smallest gesture becomes endowed with a significance that makes it mythic. Thus a poem about riding on her father's shoulders becomes larger, pushes at the doorway of an important revelation. "This is how I imagine children are shown the world," she writes, "their ankles held tight in their fathers' hands." A poem about an ancestor who burns the hens and his wife's wedding dress, apron, and tea towels with them, leads to the conclusion: "Like the dry cracking of feather and bone it is / immolation and birth most remembered." She convinces me of the truth of this assertion, and I, too, begin to remember.

It's hard to get away with this kind of assurance, but Aislinn does because of the finely faceted worlds she creates for us. When I read her poems, I can't help but think of the concluding couplet of one of John Thompson's ghazals: "If I ask questions, you'll show me / some beautiful thing you have made."

What We Have

There is no pure history, only a mess of it, a muddling
and like soup—Agnes taking this and that from the garden,
adding broad beans and chicken stock, stirring—
everything together arrives. The family at the dinner table
say nothing. But if who we are was known, traceable,
as in a straight stalk of wheat, from root to chaff,
then we could say this is the gleaning of our history,
here is the one church, our sins and glories ascribed
to that country, there. We could give them conversation,
the timbre of a voice.

Her kneading left flour dust on the breadboard,
round finger marks the only certainty in a place so new.
In the morning there are fresh loaves and treacle on the table.
Outside Agnes is sowing, and the goose makes for her loose hem,
just missing. The children watch from the kitchen, giggle,
one of the girls pressing her nose against glass.
Our history is in between their thoughts and gestures,
still as yet to be made. It is like the moment bread rises in the oven
before settling back in on itself. It is what we break open.

Sunday and the family sets out with baskets to lunch
along the strand. Seven of them in a small boat, cresting.
Over grey-capped waves, silt stirred up from the bottom, they row.
If the water was clear, we could dip our hands into the whirl
to taste it. Dry wet palms on the picnic basket, recount unerring
what we know. Rather they move with the boat as it rolls,
and let list for a moment between shores. They are neither
here nor there and in no hurry, the sough of the strait
a low whistle around them. When the boat sways again
they will pick up the oars, the slice and pull of moving forward.

Christening

A well out past the rickety grey rot-wood barn,
yoke to help balance two tin buckets of water,
marks red as the lash left across your shoulders
felt well into supper that evening,
when your father swung the axe at the main post
and you, mouth full of string beans
heard the slow death-moan of stubborn rafters;
and although he built a paddock,
a small flap-door hen house, there was always
short grass, and mud, border of thistle bush
where the barn once stood.

One January he burned the hens alive and her
wedding dress, white apron, tea towels with them.
His thin hair frozen to his head with sweat
and winter; as on the night you were born
when he ran into the flat wheat field and stayed there
slamming his fist into the snow.
Like the dry cracking of feather and bone it is
immolation and birth most remembered:
coming out into the sharp farmhouse air,
her blood cold on you, even then.

Thanksgiving

My cousin and I in the living room
at our grandparents' house,
down on our knees by the fireplace,
it's near winter and the blue-flame comes
in licks off the logs, entertainment for hours.
Then we play spin the bottle, the way children
who don't know any better will,
making silly dares, badgering each other,
sneaking into the kitchen to steal cutlery
from the already set table; a Viking hoard
under the sofa by five p.m.

Our holidays together, Hockey Night in Canada
blaring in the den, my father and uncle
sprawled out in the lazy-boy chairs.
My mother on the front porch, smoking.
Thanksgiving always stuck in the seventies
in memory, my aunt invariably wearing
an orange satin blouse, quilted slippers,
my mother's hair pinned in fat curls
she styled from hot rollers.

My cousin and I sneak into the bedroom,
with the crystal bowl of scotch mints
we stole from the uppermost cupboard,
and the commemorative bell
from our grandparents' silver anniversary.
Brian holding the tear-drop chime
to keep it from ringing.
In the closet we perform the Eucharist

again and again, kneeling
between suits, the rough tweed
of my grandfather's winter coat;
we ring the bell, place the white mint,
smaller than a wafer, in the other's mouth.
The sugar disintegrating until the soft centre
is all that remains, a pearl on the tongue
we suck at, swallow.

This was sacrament and more than once
we emerged from the closet
with an empty crystal bowl, white stains
on our fingers and thumbs.
Called back in the kitchen where adults
stand in circles, mock-angry at the lack of cutlery,
Grandpa feigning a threat to take us over his knee.
Our joy at the consternation, at getting away
with it for so long.

Communion was our secret and we held it
as close and tight as that bell, put it in
memory where it belonged,
a cherished endeavour at adulthood
like wearing a parent's clothes,
the shoes flying off your feet at the first step.
It was only later, when Brian became an altar boy,
and I went up into the hayloft
with Christopher Matthews,
that we felt ashamed, remembered
the heavy coat hanging over our heads
like a priest in his robe, although there was no
offer of benediction, only hands
reaching out, fumbling in the dark.

Shoulders

My father must have carried me on his shoulders,
although I don't remember. There are so many photos
of my sister in his arms or slung over his shoulder
and one in his red convertible when she was two or three
and he'd set her in the passenger seat. Autumn in Sudbury,
a few yellow leaves scattered over the upholstery.

I have my own memory of leaves that must have come
from a good height, how else could I have reached them?
Tugging and twisting at the stems, pulling by the fistful
those mottled flags, ruby-brown spans twice the width
of my hand. Where did I learn the names of trees,
who showed me the cocoons of caterpillars, let me touch
those white gauzy strands, luminescent tightropes
strung between fingers?

This is how I imagine children are shown the world,
their ankles held tight in their fathers' hands
as they lean and lean forward, reach out between branches,
the canopy of leaves swirling above and the small
dark eyes of birds, watching. The whole world in that space,
in the way I imagine my father carrying me on his shoulders,
stepping left then right as if dancing.

Why is it I only look up in recollections, at hands and sky
instead of feet? I remember the brown elbows of branches
mid-waltz above me, the spin and whirl as I turned,
sunlight in oblong patterns. A snapshot. I remember
that childhood as if from a great height, the smell of moss
and dust, a thatched nest in the crooked neck of the tree,
the ground coming up to greet me years before I was ready.

Climbing Lessons

Hand over hand I climbed the ladder of my grandfather's body,
the leg braces under his brown trousers, like steps
to a tree house, the only way up—the arch of my bare foot
finding the metal circle around his ankle, my toes curling over it,
that thin band as familiar as a favoured pair of shoes.

Then my left knee making for his lap, for the top of his leg brace,
leverage to haul myself up by, like our dog's collar,
how one summer, she pulled me, holding on, up a hill.
There was never any turning back, no getting hoisted by the arms.
In my grandfather's house you did things of your own volition.

His hand a compass, the way he would tap his chest, say "come here"
as I crawled over mountains to see him, to stretch out
in the hammock of his arms, bury my head between shirt and cardigan.
The thrum of his heart in my ear, intake of breath like wind
at the tent flaps. And I waited there, eyes closed,

made mental lists of the provisions I would need to get home.
The cuff of his sweater a handhold, the pleats of his pants a kind of rope.
It was up there I said my prayers before sleeping, never sure
of where we were as he walked around the house. That darkness
like a country I wanted to enter.

Sometimes the rain came like hands tapping on the roof, and too
the trickling stream of runoff from the gutters, all the sounds of the house
close, wrapped around us like a blanket. While outside the porch light
shone like a sun busy in other hemispheres. My grandfather moving
into the place beyond it, long after I'd climbed down.

The Poet's House

The dog lopes up ahead
stops every second bush,
at the burgeoning heather

lifting his leg even though
we've been walking so long
it seems he's nothing left.

And we are circling
around the far fields
afraid of turning in,

the path to your cottage
something we pass, time
and again, as if entering that house

will be the one thing we ever do.
As if it will change us.
The dog and I

know better. But if this
is the last taste of the common place
bramble and gorse,

the tangle of yellow buds
becoming caught birds
in brown nests of calyx,

the soft ripple of their wings
like fur under my hand
when the dog comes to stand beside me—

then at least let's raise it up,
watch it take leave
like a thousand everydays lifting

or open it like a door
we think nothing
of entering.

In Leaving Ireland, What Is Lost

The Irish landscape has marked our bodies.
History written on our flesh as if we were vellum.
It is like the Bufo toad, sloughing off, swallowing his skin,
layers thin as rice paper adhere to the lining of his mouth.
And we swallow our own skin, tongues
moving thick in mouths from so much living.
We are drinking that green country every day.
A toad tasting what it means to be a toad.
Swamp and lily, his own poison.

Night Train to London

Examining your hands, you slowly turn them over,
touch one, then the other, fingers pressing gently into palms.
Eight hours ago they were buried in the North Sea,
off the coast of Aberdeen—third oil rig to go up this year.
First time you were dropped from a helicopter,
to a boat a mile from the explosion.
From far away you say the water seemed littered
with the light of campfires.
Between them you reached over the side of the Zodiac,
searching for bodies, finding five.

Only twenty-nine years old and already you feel your skin
tighten, close in on your body.
Hands still sore and burning from the cold.
I touch them, ask too many questions.

At Newcastle you try to change the conversation,
until we give in to silence. The train is surging on to London.
But I keep going back—your arms lost in the blackness of the sea.
I want to release you, a stranger, as if I can pull you on board,
grab the back of your jacket, haul you in.
But we are both in that body of water now.
And beyond the window the blur of city lights
as if lighthouses in the distance, tiny pyres we pass by,
look to, but cannot reach.

Sage Hill

In the valley the wind has its own measure,
courses down to burrow the old river bottom,
splays the spear grass, the brome,
wends them into cowlicks, spun stalks,
weather vanes.
         And the hill above
is the slumbering body of a man
who went out through stable doors
carrying the lantern of the moon,
who cut across the prairie leaving rifts
in his wake.

He has come home from the war,
a battered suitcase held together with rope,
a lost letter, he has come home
and his wounds have made him
more than he was, have made him
         a barrow,
the wind over the fields,
the railway cutting through, steel tracks,
the long sight of a gun, wheat pressed out
in all directions.

Lying down in the grass he counts the passing
sparrows, waits for them to circle back, land.
He watches the glinting sun on wings,
works his hands into the cracked earth,
cups roots in his palm,
         sage and thistle
sentinel around him,

the valley a cut-away, birch-treed trench
at his feet.

When he finally goes to ground
the birds will stutter and land, fold their wings
over him, they will know him,
as if he'd always been there,
                    a gently sloping hill,
fossils, fox hole, blood stone,
under the burl of milk vetch,
under rock cress and yarrow.

Brad Cran

Brad Cran is a poet, essayist, and the publisher of Smoking Lung Press. His writing has appeared in *Songs I Used to Chase Rye* (Smoking Lung), *Hot Rods & Grasshoppers* (Smoking Lung), the *Vancouver Sun*, the *Utne Reader*, *sub-TERRAIN*, and *Geist*, where he is a contributing editor. He has attended the Banff Centre for the Arts and has read his poetry in cities across Canada. His first book (as editor), *Hammer & Tongs: A Smoking Lung Anthology* (Arsenal Pulp/ Smoking Lung), was launched at the 1999 Vancouver International Writers' Festival. For five memorable months in 1999, he co-managed the Impresario, Vancouver's first illegal drinking establishment dedicated to the promotion of Canadian culture and the humiliation of the Vancouver Police Department. Cran lives in Vancouver, where he is working on his first book of poetry and planning his comeback as a booze can proprietor.

YOU REMEMBER THE FINE ONES

Brad Cran sat around the table with fourteen other students registered in my second-year poetry workshop at the University of Victoria. He was a big guy in a red baseball cap, and when I asked the group why they wanted to study poetry, Brad replied that he'd bombed out in the fiction segment of the introductory class last year, and he'd been turned on to poetry by Patrick Lane. He's here because he flunked fiction, I thought, feeling weary and predicting we'd have a long, painful year together, wrestling with poetry. Not that being turned on by Patrick wasn't a good sign, but if a gifted salesman can sell fridges to Eskimos, as the old cliché goes, Patrick can sell poetry to the Irish.

My first impression of Brad couldn't have been more wrong. One of the delights of teaching is to watch new insights actually light up the faces of your students. This happened with Brad again and again until he was actually charged with poetry. You get used to recommending books to students and later discovering that they haven't bothered to go to the library and read them. Brad, on the other hand, not only read any books I suggested, he *bought* them. He quickly became known among his fellow students as the proud owner of the best poetry library in town, and he didn't hesitate to lend the books to his growing group of admirers.

And as for his poetry—midway through our first year together, I knew he was gifted. There was such a healthy energy in his work, such a daring as he took on topics that disturbed and potentially offended primmer sensibilities than his own. Like Al Purdy's, his poems didn't hesitate to break the family china, to throw a beer bottle at the moon, to find the beauty in imperfection, the loneliness in love. And he was only in his early twenties.

In 1996, with two other young writers, Brad founded Smoking Lung Press to publish chapbooks written by themselves and four other students who were ready for publication. They commissioned a tattoo artist to design a logo, borrowed money, and put in the endless hours of love and labour necessary to produce good books. *Geist* called their efforts "a fine expression of the small press at its best." When the other two co-founders moved away, Brad continued as the chief editor of Smoking Lung. In the fall of 1999, he edited an anthology of their best. *Hammer and Tongs*, published by Arsenal Pulp, was launched to great excitement at the Vancouver International Writers' Festival. Brad is one of those go-getters who makes things happen for his generation; he's brought into print for the first time writers who are the future of our country's literature.

Five years after our first meeting, I'm delighted to present Brad's new poetry in this anthology. He has leapt onto another level of poetic achievement, mastering the long line, writing poems distinguished by a delicacy of rhyme and rhythm, a refreshing authenticity, and a self-effacing wit. The insights, and they are numerous, are both profound and hard-won. The speaker in the travel poems sees the world he's entered without the "slightest sense / to turn away and not look back." As a result, the poems, which follow in the footsteps of Earle Birney's travel narratives, are confessional in the best possible sense, revealing the shameful and the sacred in this sojourner's encounters with what is not home. They're so well written the reader feels complicit, pulled into the lovely cadence of the lines.

"Years die hard but you remember the fine ones," he writes, "the places of beauty. . . ." Yes, I say, I remember those places and I search with him for the words that mean home. Whether they're about travel, a childhood friend who died of an overdose, or the end of love, Brad's poems dig beyond the surface to reveal what is flawed and human in all of us. They're muscular and tender and musically rich. A new voice to be grateful for.

Hitching

Catching a ride with a truck driver
heading to your hometown
is like reeling in a marlin
but it's the string of pan fries
that keeps you going.
Maybe you get lucky,
hook an overage X-hippie
driving a Beemer,
wanting to talk glory days.
Maybe he'll ask
when your last meal was,
slip you some cash and tell you
to keep the faith,
keep on rollin'
and you know you have
given him something
and you don't
feel so bad casting out your thumb,
flashing your smile,
wanting to throw stones
at the drivers as they slip away,
their eyes still pools
far from where you think
you're going.

Death of a Friend by Overdose

He looked passed out, too many pills and whiskeys
and I wanted to pull a jiffy marker from the kitchen drawer,
   draw a moustache
on his face and call out to the rest, come quick, look
what Jeff's done now, the dumb-ass is all blue and cold and dead.
Last week he pissed in my sink full of dishes. Now this?
We should shave his eyebrows and tie his shoelaces together,
strip him naked and Saran Wrap him to a stop sign,
take his picture to stick on the refrigerator,
or just soak his hand in warm water. Can't corpses still piss?
Maybe we should put him in a shopping cart and push him
to his parents' doorstep and ring the bell then run,
leave a note saying: *Sorry but we could never stop him anyhow,*
in fact we loved him for excess. Keep him like this it's all he's become.
We'd love to stay but our stars are burning fast and dumb.

Winter in a Seaside Home

Mornings are the worst. Dropping
your feet onto the cold hardwood
floor. Wondering if it's worth
the trouble: getting dressed, a cup of coffee,
finishing yesterday's paper but it's another
world far from the daily chores.
Dragging your ass through the yard,
shovel in hand, clearing out the drive
until the next snowfall. Close by
the ocean moves, salt and seaweed,
a flying gull, perhaps a pod of whales
off the point but that doesn't matter
now. All that's left you carry inside
and there is just enough time to split
the kindling for the evening fire
that you will build with care,
watching the flames, cracking
the bottle of rye you had always
hidden from her inside
your wool socks and you think
better that she left now,
better in the dead of winter,
love being the solitary occupation
that it is.

Patterns of Leaves

It's the lack of sadness that makes you want to cry.
No emotion or brother to hug. When you scream
the sky turns black and without stars.
A single pinhead of light that shines from the bar atop the hill.
Carry yourself to a thousand countries.
Pack your life into a dream the size of a pearl.
There are girls and treasure for all. Your wallet
cannot hold another bill. Take an interest in wildlife.
Comb the beach for the perfect shell. Lie on your back
and feel the wind with your toes. The trees rattle.
Crack your knuckles like a king.
Some leaves float to the ground as graceful as canoes
turning through a gentle stream. Others fall
and disappear like shooting stars into a crumpled universe.
A pile of leaves. Your amazement at how they fall.
A drunkenness you feel in your chest.
The wind running through your toes
and anything else you care to consider
can be done here.

Spider's 3 a.m.
for Adam

Here is the art of stopping the world with the cheapest rum
sold between this bar and the tip of Orion's sword.
Cut the palm trees out of your life, there is bad music and no girls for all.
Carry a torch through memories of concrete and rain, rats
and a landlady you buried in damp earth, her ruby smile
traded for the smoke singing up from the ashtray and into your good eye.
The taste of copper stings your tongue. You pull a molar from your mouth
and pay the bar in gold. Men call you sir and ask for work.
You lie and say yes. You lie and say no. Nothing is clear in your mind.
You've been gone too long and don't remember where you belong.
The lies eat away at your spine. The only thing you know is this bar is home.
Spider webs and camouflage draped along the walls.
A trough of a pisser that drizzles sadder than rain.
A bald man named Spider asleep behind the bar.
On the wall a calendar girl smiling at you
from another month you can no longer recall.

The Tenant's Song

You're married to chores. Thick peel of an onion.
Cold shine of a knife. Your landlady drops coins in your tears.
She wishes for another year. Your tongue numbs with sadness.
Hers and yours but there is nothing left to say.
Her house shakes in minor wind. Your heart an empty thought
rattles in your chest like dice. Bluffed and out-bid,
you've gambled your life away but can't leave the table.
The dishes are done and your credit is no good. Faith has made
  you dumb.
Falling down. Mid-flight without a floor to land on.
You've been falling for years and your heart hasn't caught up.
Rent is past due. Another conversation about love.
An extension of lease. More time to work things out.
And the winter rains seeping through the roof,
drown you with thoughts that sting like gasoline. Like an onion
cut beneath your eye without your slightest sense
to turn away and not look back.

You Dream of a Place

You dream of a place where sleep falls from trees
and steam rises from the jungle floor. Warm wind
massages your back and never turns to slap your face
with the rudeness of an unforgiving winter.
Forget your sins and boil your pride until it floats
towards the sun and rains down with less need
to drown you with expectation. You were born
to giggle like a salamander in a rippling stream.
The darkness of clouds curdles your curiosity
until there is nothing in your mind but rain. Go back to the dream.
The smell of wildflowers as thick as crushed berries.
Slippery stones and fallen waterfalls that tell the time
of erosion. You've been standing in line
for a decade that gave you no new love.
Rocks are shifting. Somewhere the jungle's canopies rise.
When you squeeze your eyes shut you feel
the whole world shift into a time
you see with the clarity of a vagabond
who says at last, this will do.

Tides

You walk to the beach and don't write her name in the sand.
As you didn't yesterday or didn't ever. You swim behind a fisherman
who holds his breath long enough to spear two fish
which he strings to his belt like medallions.
Thirty to forty fish, still alive, swimming back
in on themselves. They could be human ears
or a string of young rabbit. It makes no difference
to the taste of salt. The flow of blood. The feeling
of being swallowed by the depth of Ocean,
swept over reefs, coral breaking in your hand,
kicking with all your might, the tide
like a string slipped through your cheek
pulling you from the shore, towards days of storm,
the crash of waves, the lack of breath,
the hollowness of your chest that knocks
like an empty hull of a ship that has spilled its cargo
across a hundred miles of beach,
even the sand, slick with memory.

Roseau, Dominica

At the bottom of the gorge, below the waterfall,
you realize your sense of beauty has been callused.
The hummingbird with opal wings nothing more
than a distraction from cynicism. The hike back
through the jungle a testament toward green.
The small town and cobblestone streets that turn silver
with rain. In your mind it becomes a question of beauty.
How when you return the cruise ship will be harbourside.
That worst time of day. Not rage or anger but an annoyance
brought on by ignorance. Yours or theirs. The shit they buy,
how for that four hours you'll be pegged as a tourist.
It'll take you five drinks to become sentimental again
and you'll quit smoking next year. If you could be bothered
you'd stand at the pier and shout them across the ocean
to an oblivion you will hopefully never know.

Tourist is a stupid word for yourself.
Somewhere back home a man is working
your job that you never had. If you think hard enough
he's married your wife, bought your dog and taken your seat
at the local hockey game. Sometimes you just wish
for a definition of home in one word.
Years die hard but you remember the fine ones,
the places of beauty, words you expect others to know.
How you speak in local dialects and return home,
in some ways, wishing you never left. Two years since
a Christmas in the cold. Rum tastes sweetest
in the heat and you've borrowed your last few
days on bad credit. Still there is a triumph in every way of life.
Tonight you'll bunk in a hammock,

a few metres from the beach.
Tomorrow will be another day
where you choose your sins
by the wind and tide and a feeling
that you should now be moving on.

Tremors

Walls of wood bend like palm trees in hard wind
as your world shakes itself clean of ingratitude.
Here hurricanes kick down doors to remind you
permanence is perceived only through the snapshot
of a human life. A tremor is a moment of terror
that restores your lust for humour and the women
who swim off the rocks at Sunset Beach.
Never has it been more convincingly proven
that dancing is the nature of the heartbeat.
The frightened walls bending the building
shake you like a parrot in a swinging cage
in the hands of an owner who carries you
from the market to home where he may or may not
set you free.

Suzanne **Buffam**'s poems have appeared in various Canadian periodicals, including *Poetry Canada, Saturday Night,* the *Malahat Review, Grain, Prairie Fire,* and *Prism International.* Her poems have also been included in the anthologies *Breathing Fire: Canada's New Poets* (Harbour, 1995) and *Language Matters* (Oxford University Press, 1996). In 1998 she won the poetry prize in the CBC / *Saturday Night* Canadian Literary Awards. A number of the poems printed here were first read on CBC Radio's "Between the Covers" last winter, in conjunction with this prize.

THE HUM AND BUZZ OF THE WORLD

Suzanne Buffam was one of the youngest writers that Patrick Lane and I included in *Breathing Fire*, a national anthology of poets under thirty years old. It came out in 1995 and created quite a stir because it brought together so many shining talents of the new generation. Since its publication, several of the writers have gone on to garner national attention, including Stephanie Bolster, who won the Governor General's Award in 1998, and Suzanne, who won the CBC's national award for poetry in 1998. I wonder if she's the only one to have received such a major poetry prize before publishing her first book. Whatever the case may be, she has now created high expectations that I'm sure she'll fulfill.

Suzanne was in one of the first classes I taught at the university when I arrived in Victoria eight years ago. What a feisty, smart young woman she was. Once when we were moving tables and chairs to set up a classroom for the workshop, I made a teasing remark about her using her Fine Arts degree to become a furniture mover. "Oh, no," she replied, "it's your job I'm after." Even at the time, I knew she was someone to contend with.

When you meet so many talented students over the years as a writing teacher, you can't help but wonder why some go on to do the kinds of things that Brad, Aislinn, and Suzanne are doing, and others, equally gifted, disappear. In Suzanne's case, I think that her passionate pursuit of writing might have something to do with the support of her family. Working with me on a directed studies project on the prose poem, she set up her research paper as a dialogue with her father. His questions were the kind that would be posed by a bright, literate man who didn't know a lot about poetics but who was interested because it was a such a large part of his daughter's life. In trying to track down Suzanne to include her in this book, I had to phone her parents in

Vancouver to find out her number in Iowa, where she's studying. Her father, when told the reason, acted like the best of literary agents. He got in touch with his daughter and made sure she got back to me. He also told me on the phone that she was almost too busy in her studies to write and he hoped she'd get back to poetry. I felt a twinge of envy—imagine having a father who wants you to write poetry!

You can understand why he's encouraged his daughter to pursue what many parents would consider an insecure career. She's so good at what she does. The first thing I'm struck by is the intelligence in her poems. Many of them are maps of the mind as it moves quickly and adeptly through "the hum and buzz of the world" and tries to find form and meaning. This is particularly evident in the love poems. Although literature abounds with personal addresses to a beloved, love poems are especially hard to write. How do you move beyond the worn-out language of romance?

Suzanne does this by paying close attention to what's out there, whether it be near or cosmic, and by never turning away from the complexity of both human emotions and things, from a "wasp, waist-deep, headlong / inside a bitter grape" to "a vain extravagance of stars." Along with emotional depth, her poems emit a peculiar kind of purity, a sense that each word has been held to the light of the mind and has taken on its sheen. As in the writing of Phyllis Webb and Louise Glück, there's a luminous intelligence that's a delight to behold.

The Garden

1. Profusion

How the winged ants and the honeybees,
large and dark as human eyes, the butterfly
clapping its wings on the branch like a bat,
the heather, the mint, the bronchial
vines of the grapes, and the maple

cohere. How simple
the garden, in its lucid confusion, the mind
in the plummet of sleep: no need
to remember, no need to forget—
just the hum and the buzz of the world,

begetting. As though by paying close enough
attention to the garden, I might
join it. As though I might relinquish
this slavish devotion to intention and begin,
at last, to mean something, the way

the wasp, waist-deep, headlong
inside a bitter grape
means business. There is no simple way
to say this. I am simply
abuzz with instincts

I cannot comprehend. And my head
gets in the way of everything, the way the house
gets in the way of everything outside.

2. Intent

There is an opposite of memory that is not
simply forgetting but
attention. When she does not think
about him, very likely

she is thinking: "How the winged ants
and the honeybees," "How simple," "the way the wasp,
waist-deep, headlong inside a bitter
grape."

Very likely she is counting
to a hundred, while the garden
goes about its humming like a dizzy field of atoms
she can't enter. She may

have an end result in mind, and not yet know it,
or else she knows it all too well and yet is willing
—and is working—to deny it.
Very likely she is hoping

to forget him, the way the wind,
at rest above the garden will forget
—without forsaking it—
to scuff the glassy surface of the pond.

What Is Called Déjà Vu

Rain taps little circles in the pavement that glisten, briefly,
then vanish. Your fingers
tap along my spine.
A slant wind. Eavestroughs.

The world rises wet and self-evident from the floor of the mind.
Far off, the sound of a train
forging into its whistle unspools
a wake of old longings. The box opens in

on itself like a dream inside which a crouched
animal is awaiting
release, recognition.
Its little teeth glisten.

Hunter's Moon

Outside, a white mist spreads across the lawn.
Wind strips the maple to a barren nest.
A woman calls you from your other life.

Her message on the answering machine is an attempt
to forge from grief a sturdier resolve.

It would be easy to identify with her. To say,
"That could be me, one day," or, "Now
she will hang up the phone, go into the bathroom and stare
at her face in the mirror a long time."

In this way I get to know her
better than I know myself.

It would be easy to resent her.
The way she needs you more than I
am willing to allow myself.

As though you had saved her life one day and now
you are responsible for it. Because you are a man,
and kind, you need

to call her back. In another life you would be
hunting deer across the close-cropped fields.

There would be light
to guide you home.

The Crosswalk

I walked out in the early evening calm
and crossed the narrow street despite the sign
forbidding me to cross: *Don't walk / Don't walk /*
Don't walk, its voice an angry orange glare
that stammered, steadied, held, and finally, broke

mid-sentence, as a man, watching a woman
walk away from him, across a narrow
side-street into darkness, will finally break
his stare and blink up blindly at the light.
Fine, he'll say (the flame burns white when hottest), *walk.*

Shapes at Midnight

Across the street the artists are still working in their studios.
I can see them through my curtains, moving intermittently
towards and then away from the assorted shapes
and colours on the walls, each private artist vibrant in her cell.

On the second floor, a woman reaches out her hand
as though to grasp a rectangle of blue and reposition it, a careful
movement, full of a new love of ideas and distrust
of the heart. At the last second, before her hand connects
with the colour and commits, she draws it back
and runs it slowly through her hair.

Now she stands there, in the centre of her studio,
lit starkly by the swinging bulb above her and bisected
by the open window's wooden sash. Her hand
hangs in mid-air. Hoisted in the branches of the maple,
the moon flags at half-mast.

               It is the moon that dropped
behind the poplars last November, when you
first introduced me to this version of despair: halfway
we cannot bear and yet it's here
we long to stay: the artists in their studios, the sentimental
rectangles of blue, the moon, the ramifying
branches of the maple through the window, halfway
between the woman I am watching
and myself, beginning at this hour to lose green.

Inside the Hours

I scrape the dregs of dinner down the sink
and fill the sunken metal tub with suds.
The muted, underwater thud of cups
against a shallow saucepan's chrome
mimics the body's blunted throb
within the muffling blood. The man
beside me in the kitchen drinks
his wine and watches slender legs
slide down the fluted glass. He doesn't ask
me where I've been or where it is I go
when evening locks us snug as spoons
inside their spoon-shaped groove.
(The top-left drawer they're stored in
sticks; we have to slam it like a door.)
For all I know, he knows. For all I know,
he goes there too. The blue clock on the wall
is starred with flecks of incandescent light;
innumerate, its pocked face shines
a ticking disk of unrelenting night. I rinse each
moss-green plate and pass it to him clean.

Late in the Season

Indian summer and the evening warm enough to wander
home through, sleeveless down the centre of the unlit street.
The breeze shot through with a few pale threads of fall.
Planets ripe and orange as the berries on the neighbour's mountain ash.

Above the drooping spirits of hydrangeas, a vain extravagance
of stars: there is nothing more to wish for from the season.

And so, at night, I dream again of winter, the city locked
in a suit of lucid armour like the heart, seen through to.
The bare trees sheathed in so much beauty it will break them
when they are most strong.

And when I wake, it is to daylight, the blade of understanding
pressing gently at my throat. You are not coming. Last winter
was a gift I am only now beginning to receive.

The Onset

Farewell to insects, farewell
to the numerous
finches, to wandering coatless
under "the palm-
sized leaves of the maple."

Turn up your collar, sharpen
your intellect, prepare
again for hunger . . .
If only the body
could make up its mind. If only

the river
flowed in a single direction—
but there goes a bottle,
caught on the chop
of a wave pushing north,

back into current,
wind-fuelled, retracing,
while the depths plough south
toward candour.
In winter the river

will lock like a door. Too late, Too late,
the wind in the branches
will chant, but today,
bright aberration,
brief check in the chain

of events leading up to
decision, the wind
is lifting the fallen leaves back to the trees.

Before Darkness

Empty, the dresses in the window are more beautiful.
In a stillness between thinking she remembers thinking
this. If not waiting, what then to call it?
Before darkness, after sunset, there's a window
in the day through which light passes, without
shadow, and shadow simply happens
where nothing blocks the light. The dresses
in this window wear a stillness
she thought to call its opposite. Now she
revises: she wants
to touch them. They want not to be touched.

The Rendition

Outside the perfect solitude in which
her child sleeps
as though he were not born, a woman
leans her cheek against the open
of her palm. The sunlit curtain
is satin, drawn. Another early
autumn presses hotly
at the glass. Her eyes, downcast, half-
closed against the impulse
to look up, to look away, are focused
on his face. It is completely closed.
Behind the easel, History
takes up her brush. She adds
a little colour to the cheeks.

susan musgrave

Susan Musgrave's first book of poems, *Songs of the
Sea-Witch*, was published by Sono Nis Press in
1970, when she was nineteen. She has, thirty years
later, published over twenty books (poetry, fiction,
non-fiction, and juvenile)—the most recent being
Things That Keep and Do Not Change (poetry;
McClelland and Stewart, 1999). A long personal
essay, "Junkie Libido," was included in *Desire in Seven
Voices*, edited by Lorna Crozier (Douglas and
McIntyre). In January 1999, she and her husband,
Stephen Reid, were profiled on the CBC's *Life and
Times*, in an hour-long documentary titled "The Poet
and the Bandit." In 2000 Beach Holme will publish
*What the Small Day Cannot Hold: Collected Poems 1970-
1985*, and Knopf her third novel, *Cargo of Orchids*.

In 1996 Musgrave received the Tilden (CBC /
Saturday Night) Canadian Literary Award for Poetry,
and the Vicky Metcalf Short Story Editor's Award. In
1999 her children's book, *Dreams Are More Real Than
Bathtubs* (illustrated by Marie-Louise Gay) was
selected by the Canadian Children's Book Centre for
Our Choice 1999-2000.

Al Purdy Took a Bus to the Town
Where Herodotus Was Born

"The town we visited," Al says, "remember
the town—we caught a bus there."
Eurithe can't remember the name of the place,
either, but she recalls a wake-up call
and a foreign voice saying, "Your cold breakfast
is coming up." The last time I made Al
a birthday cake it fell, but Al was gracious
enough to say *thank you for your largesse.*

There are vast areas of my —————
that are missing, for instance the name
of the restaurant in Dublin where each dish
was an approximation of its ideal,
or the Christian names of my daughter's
school bus drivers I said I'd never forget:
Mrs. Blood, Mr. Wolf, and Miss Hood.
I wanted to write a Young Adult book
about "the late bus," the one the bad kids
always took, but I didn't want my obituary
ending up in the Entertainment Section
of the newspaper where I once found a prognosis
of Elizabeth Taylor's tumour. I don't want
to be anybody's Smile of the Day
which is why I'm glad I didn't shoot myself
cleaning Henry White's house on Haida Gwaii
last summer—my death would have made
the *National Enquirer* along with Wife Used
Cheating Hubby's Toothbrush to Clean the Commode.
In Henry White's house I sucked up a .22 bullet,

heard a bang, saw sparks, and the next thing
I remember I was seeing headlines: Woman Shoots Self
in Head with Vacuum Cleaner. The photograph
of my sad brain looks like a honeydew melon
soaked in V8 Juice all night after being run over
by a train the time I went pub-hopping in Oxford
and landed in a punk bar eating drugged cookies
which I worried about later when I started
hallucinating because I was pregnant
with Charlotte and didn't want her to be born
in the corridor of British Rail while I peaked
on Peak Freen Digestive Biscuits. Mary Oliver
says poems are ropes let down to the lost, I wish
someone would keep that in mind when they ever
find me. A critic in the *Globe* asks why
poets are always *losing* things, especially
people, why can't they *find* something
instead, and I believe he deserves an answer.

"The town where they lost your suitcase," Al says,
"remember the town—we caught a bus there."
Eurithe can't remember if her luggage showed up
but she does recall a wake-up call, a foreign
voice saying, "Your hour has come," and the line
going dead. You cherish people
then they are gone: what more can be said
about the ones I'd rather be with,
the ones I love best.

I thank them for their largesse.

Carnal Garage

The day I won the Nobel Prize
for Peace, my mother was arrested
for stalking Knowlton Nash. The day
I woke up to find there were no drugs
in the house was the day I stopped coping
with reality. When I took up reading
contemporary poetry of bereavement I changed
my mind about being happy I hadn't blown off
the Cliffs of Moher in County Clare in 1972,
I wouldn't be sitting here poking the eyes out
of a potato if that had been the case, would I?

Try to describe grief. If only there was a day
when my daughter would not leave
that picture of herself on her father's bed
with "Hi, Dad, remember me?" written on it.
If only he would remember to notice,
even once, it might make a difference. But Dad's
on the nod again, smudging the Winnebago
and I'm all done with the I'm sorry's,
I only wish I could help you out of this.

Anne Boleyn was the first woman
I ever looked up to, it takes balls
to say *the executioner is, I hear, very expert*
and my neck is very slender when
the hangman says *no noose is good noose*,
like every anaesthetist I've known who thinks
cracking bad jokes is the way to put you under.
It takes *cojones* the size of coconuts

to lose your head while all around you
are keeping theirs, doing the housework,
ejaculating prematurely, oh, yes, I'm coming

down hard, what is it, you ask, I love most
about my life? Is it possible to be
honest? Behaviour doesn't just happen, you say,
there are always underlying causes. But who
can handle it? In "Applying Biblical Truth"
I read it is helpful to see people as having
some of the characteristics of icebergs,
and that "Christians are like a tea-bag."
Shouldn't it be "Christians are like tea-*bags*?"

Metaphor frightens me. Last night
at my Al-Anon meeting one woman talked
about moving the large rocks off her vacant lot
and getting up in the morning to see
a whole bunch of smaller rocks she hadn't
noticed before because the larger rocks
were in the way, and I was the only person
in the room who didn't know the rocks
were supposed to be problems. I mean
I was thinking, why didn't she just hire
a fucking bulldozer to get rid of *all* the rocks
at once, but everyone else was nodding
like they *knew* rocks stood for something
that stands in our way. I could never be
a heroin addict because I can't stand
doing the same thing day after day.
Grief is the price we pay

for love, you try to say, but as of today
I'm all out of love, and its subsidiaries.
Behaviour doesn't just happen but I can't handle it
when it does. Two years in maximum security
is the price my mother paid for trailing Knowlton
and his bedroom eyes all the way to Africa.

Try to describe sorrow. When I found
my lover's new sunglasses face-down
in the gravel, the lenses smashed out, two
half-eaten Snickers bars blocking the toilet,
a wallet greasy with money, I felt sad at last,
I felt everything was over. Wrong again,
it was only a new beginning. But
every time I find another C-note on the floor
I make a contribution to the Kill for Peace
in Kosovo Organization which is how I won
the Nobel Prize, by saving all the proceeds
of a slipping down life I found scattered
around the house, enough to make Milosevic come
to his senses: I took him to my carnal garage
and gave him a chance to experience what
Canadian women are famous for. After *that* he said
war wasn't doing it for him any more, killing
wasn't giving him what he needed. The day I won

the Nobel Prize for Peace I blew up
in front of the television. I couldn't take it
any more, my mother being front page news
also, and everybody looking for answers
as if by stopping the war in Kosovo
I should have been able to stop

my mother. Later I made a statement
about the aging inmate population in America,
more prisoners dying of heart attacks than from
the electric chair/gas chamber/firing squad
put together. Try to describe a fist a split
second before it hits your lip, or the way
a syringe sucks up blood, or the quiet death
a person sometimes comes to: what happens
to plum blossom after spring snow?
Try to describe love—what other word
might there have been for it? I know now there is
no greater loneliness than in its brief shining.

Fran Bourassa

F**ran Bourassa** grew up in a small town in the
Châteauguay Valley in Quebec. After her
parents separated, Fran and her sister spent two years
being raised by Catholic nuns in a convent. They
were reunited with the rest of the family, now a
blended family of seven children, when her father
remarried. At seven years old, Fran learned to speak
English, the language of her stepmother. Shortly
after the marriage, her birth mother died an
alcoholic. Fran has just begun to show her work
outside her own community, starting last year as
delegate for the BC Festival of the Arts. She feels
lucky to have met the poets who have helped her
along the way. Fran thanks Chris Patton, Don
McKay, Patrick Lane and the Moberly poets, the
Voices group, and especially, Susan Musgrave.

POETRY STEPPING INSIDE HER

Fran Bourassa enrolled in my weekend poetry workshop in the fall of 1999, at Sechelt. She caught my attention the first day by arriving late. She soon made up for it (I never hold lack of punctuality against a poet) by regaling the group with stories Patrick Lane had told of lying naked under the cold northern lights and stars, when she took his workshop that summer in Dawson Creek.

Fran writes from places many of us have visited—the countries of love, motherhood, being somebody's lost child, grief. As she wrote in an earlier version of her bio note (and I appropriated, saying I wanted to use her words for my own purposes), "Religious imagery, themes of loss and of abandonment, are constant in her poetry." Of herself she also had this to say: "Maybe you believe, as Fran does, that everyone is given a way, a tool, or a gift to help them through life. Fran would tell you she was given poetry."

The first poem of Fran's I read was "Out in the Open," about roads not taken and other lonely roads. Her lover is described as "poetry stepping inside me," and she laments:

> Long after he has gone to sleep
> under the big belly of the night,
> too close to his young body
> I fight to keep my hands to myself . . .
> both of us old enough to know some things are
> never meant for long
> never meant to be caught or kept . . .

There are tender love poems about her father, too. In one, about the night of her conception, she imagines him one humid June, miles of slow hot road ahead, making his way back to her mother who sits by a window in the dark, a hot pink silk slip wet against her skin, waiting for him.

Her poetry makes you feel the sulky heat, hear the squeal of tires on the pepper-smelling road; we become ghosts in the empty passenger seat beside her, sharing her lust for absolution, and for the warmth of a lover's skin.

> I finish this poem that goes nowhere, is about nothing
> but how a wind can blow you in a circle . . .
> This poem
> a paper skin needing
> to be folded, shut

Bering Strait

It is my duty
to come to your death bed—
a tiny, white island
of rumpled sheets I wade to
from a sea that has always churned about us

Weary, we are both worn down by these efforts
Wary, back against the white bone cliff,
I huddle into the ribs of the chair
my own shore,
hands folded tightly as unopened letters

Shifting uneasily in
Bed. Chair.
A widening sea between us, time
passes imperceptibly as
the moving-apart of continents

Even now, I doubt
the smallness of your hand,
its stillness on the bed—
light and delicate as shell
hollow as the bones of seabirds
and the skeleton claw
of the snow crab

I watch, as your breath struggles
fluttering the covers
    a loose sail, the wave of curtain, a flight
    of paper out an open window, white

gulls on the wing—settling
suddenly on a sea, cold and gone still.

Out in the Open
for James Chiba

1.
Long after he has gone to sleep
under the big belly of the night,
too close to his young body
I fight to keep my hands to myself
Sky carries the ache of shooting stars
both of us old enough to know some things are
never meant for long
never meant to be caught or kept

The taking of lovers, he tells me
is not physical, but a foolish
wind is loose over the night field
and where the blade of the plow
has turned the earth inside out
the second crop of timothy
breaks through the scars
and is growing, unbidden
new, sweet and blue green

He is poetry stepping inside me

I watch the sun come up
pink and gold
over his sleeping face
Lost now, any chance I had
of leaving untouched

2.
All this new land,
Old, the second time around
Nowhere to go but down
south from Dawson Creek to Vancouver
Map spread out—a ghost in the passenger seat

On the way up
names of the towns were titles of poems
Now, places to put behind me, a quick stop
a hard place to kneel to check the air,
fill up at the stations and crossings

Racing the Thompson down the canyon
close to the edge
Stupid dreams of flying
him, last on my mind

Coming headlong from Lytton
into the mountains
In and out of the tunnels
Errobee, Hell's Gate, Alexandra, Sailor Bar, Saddle Rock, Yale

feels like dying again and again
underground
there is so much to wish for
to have been young and beautiful to have
a chance to take back the dry clay kiss
instead to come wet to his mouth
risking the threat of wind, frost, of being cut down

but there is no resurrection
just a rear-view mirror
a winding road
closing me to home

Now rain is a shield
a lead drape on the trees
the mean spit of the semis
Coming to, is this wet green land
these heavy clouds
miles of it follow like old grey dogs
on the heels of the coast

3.
Morning
when the rain has fallen all the stars
The map lies across my naked body
I trace the crease of mountains and wheal of river
following the red line
long to the north
put my finger where he is
the stretch wider than the spread of my hand

I finish this poem that goes nowhere, is about nothing
but how a wind can blow you in a circle
about the mean ruse of northern light

This poem
a paper skin needing
to be folded, shut

To My Father

On a humid June night all, too close
Clouds pack up against each other like testy passengers
grumbles of thunder in their throats

and you can't wait to get home
still miles of slow hot road ahead,
black quicksand under the wheels of the bus
no rain for days just the spit of stones that crack
against the windshield

She sits in the dark by the open window
Not moving away even when lightning splinters close by
Not heeding yet another storm warning, from mother or nature

Hot, the pink silk slip, turns to a wet skin against her nakedness
Her thick black hair piled high as satin cord on her head
The smoke from her cigarette escapes into the narrow street
down to the sound of the tavern she will work at after two more
   babies
and finally, take the tip and run

You, road-weary and beaten having dodged
trucks, cars and the ground floor lady's squealing children
as you climb the stairs, they spill over
the rails and steps, all as unruly
as your feelings inside, still
too hot to put them to bed
three to a cot

You duck the line of diapers, white flags
sodden as the flannel clouds, where she sees
her future surrendered
You pass your own red-haired baby,
sprawled in her crib, neglected in her sleep

But tonight, it is there you find your woman
perched against the window as if ready to fly
raw and beautiful, home
is where you rest your head
against the cool silk of her lap, your hand
finding its way to her black curling lace
and she takes you
in her dusk, her musk on you a perfume
you will never forget
and when the tight-fisted sky finally lets go its rain
wet kisses on her bare back
splash past the open window, the curtains
shivering

After the Accident

All the lights out
she watches her father
alone on the back porch
gazing through the dark
at the river moving by

He smokes his cigarette, spent
the ashes fall to the floor,
drift into the shadows
under the wheels of the chair

Sometimes can't see
the moon, smeared by a cloud

Down on the end of their dock
the one-legged crane
searches the thin black water
The moon, too, an eye
opening and closing on the water

On the other side of the river
trains rattle the night
—old bones in a jar
a bull bellows
across an empty field
a song for her father

Bird dives, a clean slice
on the skin of the still river
Sends waves through the thick silence,

across the flat of her father's stare

For a moment, both of them remembering,
the hot loud summers
small feet swinging over the edge of the dock
slapping hands together
again Daddy again
watching him fly through the air
bend in two and straighten
jack-knife
that old slow river

Visiting Hour
for Ted Willis

Blind now, he asks in my direction
about Barry's baby—huge inside me,
I pick at the books on the table,
Where Angels Fear to Tread
We speak of his girls, Nahanee, Jesse, so big now
at five and seven

And there are no more words
Language gone, a dropped stitch, a record player
unplugged, a station lost in a tunnel

After a time, his arm reaches for nothing, I see
his once-beautiful carpenter's hands,
soft and peeling as the arbutus bed he shaped for us
that brought the rust-beaten truck back to life
on the barren back road
Those hands that laid me in the bath
and washed my feet, gentle as a jesus
the first time we made love
The same hands that found for me,
in those exquisite circles, a way to come
to cry out, oh my god, under shifting sheets,
I see his belly has grown
tumours, one as big as a pumpkin,
I am suddenly self-conscious
a small foot kicks under my ribs
I look instead out the window,
the mountains green with summer
a perfectly clouded sky

The view so grand, I put it in the way
of my old love on the bottom rung of his ladder
This time, his turn to be lifted.
I find a place on his forehead for goodbye.

This is not sorrow, nor love
or charity. Not duty. Not the compassionate kiss for the leper.
I yearn for absolution, to be free
to feel satisfied our full bellies
share such opposite fates
I lust for a forgiveness
you are no longer able to give, for
packing up and stealing everything
you ever gave me, for
waiting to come to you

Elsie K. Neufeld

Elsie K. Neufeld was born into a Russian
Mennonite family that lived on a farm in the
Fraser Valley. On Sunday evenings, she and her
mother wrote letters to relatives in Manitoba,
Germany, and the USSR. Uncle Abram, a
schoolteacher exiled in Siberia, replied quickly, often
enclosing a poem or Russian fable. Elsie was hooked,
and her writing soon progressed from letters and
diaries to non-fiction articles and stories. After her
brother was killed by a drunk driver and she couldn't
find a book on sibling grief, she wrote *Dancing in the
Dark: A Sister Grieves* (Herald Press, 1990). And now,
poetry. Since taking a poetry class last winter, she
wakes to words and images, surprised but delighted
that poetry has found her.

Besides parenting three children, writing, reading,
and gardening, Elsie Neufeld teaches writing courses
in the Abbotsford area. She lives with her family on
Sumas Mountain.

THE POEM GOING ON WITHOUT US

The poet Patrick Friesen, a dear friend my daughter describes as being "even nicer than a Dad," and with other attractive, enduring qualities as well, brought Elsie Neufeld and me together. Elsie had been a student of Patrick's and wanted to continue having her work "edited" by a poet.

She e-mailed me a group of poems, and some prose, and I sent back responses to as many as I could. And then, in June of 1999, my husband went to the bank and never came back, and my life was suddenly more full of weeping than I had ever known.

Elsie was one of the first to come to my side, by e-mail, with the clearest, sweetest, softest, wisest words of comfort—not unlike her poetry. Even when she isn't trying, I thought, she makes poetry out of our joy and our grief.

There's a sense of timelessness in her work—of life going on despite its inevitable ending—and a strong sense of place. Soon after her father is felled by a stroke, her mother plants seedlings from the seeds she smuggled home on their last trip to Holland: "hollyhock growing past roofline / with leaves wide as the spread / of dad's hands,"

> and dad smiling from heaven
> waving buds into blossom red as the wine
> the two of them made on the farm
> his voice in the towering stalk, calling
> *come, let us drink one together.*

There is a quiet dignity in these poems, which range in subject from memory to portraits of prairie women at home preparing suppers of roast beef and potatoes "dirt fresh and boiled in their jackets." I think of Lorna Crozier's "The Garden Going On

Without Us." Elsie's collection could be called "The Poem Going On Without Us," because they leave us behind in another place, a sweet-sad place where we remember how life once was, or could have been. She writes, for instance, about her daughter's coming of age, and with painful and aching clarity, about blood-ties:

> the girl's twelve and becoming a woman
> chest budded and legs growing unwanted hair
>
> some days I notice my Schick shaver is dull
> its lubricated edge filled with hair not my own
> and last week she asked *when can I shave?*

Ultimately these are hopeful, life-affirming poems that weave you into their world, where they are waiting to be worn. Her poems take shape around you, the way an old sweater or jacket takes shape, and strengthen our fragile lives. As she writes in "Word into Flesh": "The way home is all words."

In the Herb Bed

echinacea spike the air with cone-heads
purple as a cough stems wired and long

the lavender bent on heather basil and dill
chives domed like poppies spent in a field

sage telling thyme its lemon curled parsley
and rosemary stretched in feverfew's shade

catmint seeding itself at tarragon's feet
bee balm hummed by a bird and oregano

Cicely sweet on Valerian while curry all night
dreams lamb's ear the borage prickly and blue

My Mother's Hollyhock

is a mutant eleven feet
seeds gleaned from a garden
in the last trip to Holland with father
and smuggled home in her purse
potted in soil then watered and
cared for as though her beloved

father felled by a stroke and she soon
moving with seedlings to a new home
her heart rooted in earth and hands
finding never enough dirt to garden

hollyhock growing past roofline
with leaves wide as the spread
of dad's hands and none wearing rust
the neighbours imagining beans
   or a pumpkin gone mad
mother bewildered

and dad smiling from heaven
waving buds into blossoms red as the wine
the two of them made on the farm
his voice in the towering stalk, calling
   come, let us drink one together

Word into Flesh

The way home is all words
the mind searching always
for shallows to cross or stones
a path to a hollow of sleep

skin filtering the air for signs
of both the dead and living
the Grandfather clock in the hall
slicing each hour into four with
gong ringing *gone! gone!*

Father's skin cells turned to
dust motes and spores
the rain on the window after dark
remembering those others
names on a list of the dead

fingers curled to make memory word
turn word into flesh the hours all night
long and longing to be lit by more
than these illuminated numbers
falling towards another mourning.

What's Memory?

sometimes I wonder what the living
remember last and the dead first ponder

father bent to the west like a sundown
a band tight on his arm like a pallbearer's
sleeve and his heart beating lines in a box
half of him frozen already and it's
not even noon his family on guard
whispering *stay* though they're wishing
he'd go go to where his dead lie in wait
his father and mother son five brothers and

friends what's memory but a key to the gates
of heaven or a magnet to draw the dead
back to life and the dying towards death
it's so hard to let go and still harder
to travel alone to a home long forgotten
or believe in one's end as beginning
his hands stiff as spent flowers

Who can define alpha omega or say
whether the hands over there are as warm
or if he remembers the feel of flesh
over bones or a pulse that last rasping

Touching Forever

the prairie is a way wide as the sky
and this road is as long as forever
land rolling itself flat all day long
and trees scrubbing the wind hollow
it's warm out here and I'm longing
for borders ocean and air it's time
to go home that's for sure and besides

I'm tired of men wearing farmer caps
the visors sweat brown and branded
with names of cow feed or the town co-op
their women at home getting suppers
of roast beef redeemed in a gravy
the colour of old butter and on the side
coleslaw squared carrots and corn

dad would have loved it the potatoes
dirt fresh and boiled in their jackets
the soft click of his teeth breaking
through skin but that was then this is now
he's gone and I'm here on the prairie road
breathing alfalfa wild roses and clover
a canola sea waving hello and goodbye
wind pulling the heads back and forth
it's stringed music everything's quiet

some days the waves are gentle as fleece
but the field is so bright it could blind you
that's when you can't help turning away
it's like a glance at the sun for too long

the land afterwards muted and as strange
as the unbroken sky its blue hanging low
but now everything's fading seems empty

blackbirds and magpie sitting on scrub bush
I like it when their wings darken the sky
orange feathers brilliant as a flash fire
song honey-sweet clear and the horizon a foil
of elevators rising high and still
higher as the lines on the road touch forever

Raining from a Blue Sky

It's raining today and the sky's mostly blue
everything's changing my daughter's breaking
out each morning scanning her face in a mirror
the girl's twelve and becoming a woman
chest budded and legs growing unwanted hair

some days I notice my Schick shaver is dull
its lubricated edge filled with hair not my own
and last week she asked *when can I shave?*
I used to sneak my brother's Gillette
time has a way of remembering us back

how we stood in line to use the washroom
the steam after bath time a wet shadow
that followed you out window held open
in a perpetual yawn with an old wooden spoon
yes, time has a way of doing us right or wrong

doesn't matter my daughter's twelve like I was
back then when becoming a woman was a book
and a secret one hid in a brown paper bag
not this a young girl wearing a bra a white
training bra from The Bay and I'm stuck

in Hooges Drygoods asking my mom for
my first one do you need one she asks
and what size a clerk in the aisle measures
my bust like I'm a doll or some line in a story
there are no secrets here or in the one-room

library across the street the librarian
wearing pearl earrings and red lipstick red
her finger a spine over her mouth
and I'm begging mom for a library card
but what if it's late will you pay?

my daughter from across the room points
at her face doesn't want me or anyone else
to see how big don't laugh I remember those days
remind her the swan was an ugly duckling
mu-uhm she says with an exclamation mark

her forehead revealed oh how times change
I'm twelve again I'm 42 and it's me all of me
she my mother and the blood ties and this
this is no lie that in the last summer of this century
it's raining from a mostly blue sky

Matthew's Point, Galiano
for Rachel and Alex

In this hour filled with wind wasp and ferry
the mind buzzes what's gone and is coming
time like the bee with its striped jacket
making this moment a prisoner of memory
a mother sits on her beach chair watching
the Queens go by scissors through silk
and the pass cut open and blasted with a two-tone
sound of a horn a long echo preceding the ship
round the bend a man on the deck whistling
to a past where sails bow to the ways of the wake
sheets billowed and white as the foam and spray
shells surfing the waves in the last lift and fall
the white bowls stacked on the sand where
two girls build castles their shells doubling
as pools and stones pressed into the fortress
jewels on a mosque and one for each pocket
the sky is a giant clam bake and everyone's
naming the clouds there's a mother goose
the skull of a bird a horse with butterfly wings
a gull catching a ride past the castles and girls
their hands smoothing the walls and six towers
a bucket of water flooding the moat and a pond
in the garden willows and oaks hung with seaweed
grass blades sharp as glass under a bench and a gate
dark as the rattle of rocks below the cloud worried sky
The Queen of Nanaimo with a bellow sliding past
while the bees buzz on and the shells clatter to shore
and the wind makes new waves and its gone gone

a fool's house and the woman's alone on the beach
in her chair as the girls whinny and gallop away
the wasps wind and ferries keeping their time.

Wanting Easter

It is Easter
and there is no lily
and I am wanting a lily
to trumpet me awake
the air thick with spice
and flower so white
its long throat heavy
and the starred tip of its tongue
yellow and wet
singing praise

ben
Perry

Benjamin Thomas Perry was born in Berlin, Germany, in 1976. He came to Canada as a migrant in 1978 and grew up in Coquitlam, a suburb of Vancouver. His father, who studies languages, told him that the word Coquitlam means "smells like salmon." Ben has been writing poetry since he was nine. He met Susan Musgrave in Masset, at the north tip of Haida Gwaii, while staying at the Copper Beech House. Last summer, Ben returned to Masset and attended what someone touted as the potlatch of the century. A large pole was erected. Currently Ben is attending the University of Victoria, taking a range of courses that someone referred to as "a walk through the garden." Benjamin Perry speaks better English than French, and better French than German. Mostly he only speaks one language, whatever that means.

LIKE THE BEST OF POETRY ITSELF

I don't go looking for poets. Poetry, yes, but not poets. So it always disturbs me when a poet shows up, in a place where I am not expecting one to be. It both disturbs and pleasantly surprises me—like the best of poetry itself.

I first heard Ben Perry read his work at David Phillips's Copper Beech Guest House in Masset, on the north coast of Haida Gwaii, two summers ago. David ran the house when I stayed there for a time in the '70s.

The night Ben read, David had prepared one of his meals for which he is island—and world—renowned. When he announced there was to be a poetry reading after huckleberry pie, my heart tried to sneak out through the soles of my feet, and the rest of my body tried to follow. No escape. I was trapped in a house with poets who had been masquerading as fellow house guests.

Feeling uncharacteristically stuffed and characteristically gloomy, I tried to disappear into an overstuffed chair as Ben began to read. His renegade energy, with much of the energy of Bob Dylan's early lyrics, soon found its way to my ear—a grab-push-pull of words and sounds guaranteed to give you anything but a black belt in boredom. He seemed fearless when he read, unsure of where he was headed in this world but trusting in his own words to take him there.

> Scorpions nest in your shoes
> And fungus grows in your hat
>
> Now trust no one but your dinner
> And don't even trust that. . . .

His poems go on drunks, have sex with anyone; they are tragic and romantic. Always in your face, they conceal a whole lot of what goes on beneath the surface, of what's hidden in sooty darkness, like "a chimney full of angry butterflies." As he writes in "From Love Bandits: Unite!":

> Precise landings are not possible for insects.
> They bounce off their targets a few times before they settle.
> A flower petal; the perfect landing site—
> spring-loaded to reduce shock on impact
> —a little trampoline.
> What a beautiful transaction.

He's shy, wild, edgy. His poetry is a rainbow crash landing in a crop circle where two bodies are making free love. And when it starts to rain, he writes, "it ain't gonna stop."

Fate of the Unguarded

The rubber son of the ancient man
Like a molten seal on a cold day
Steam rolling to the skyscraper air
Like children tripped up stairs

He'd fallen to a certain sin
The serrated knife from the taximan's tweed
Laxed his guts out like a leopard spew salad

The enemy seized the diamond
Escaped into a thicket stacked with nettle
And all that was left
Was the body of an absurd man
With glasses the thickness of my hand
Moaning a vocabulary of sleep
A monologue disjointed
And me who sat on the fence
Fidgeting

Excerpts

Number two

When you grin I think to myself that I could
stick toothpicks inbetween all your teeth

Shall we sip tea?

You can strain it.

Sip enough
   nod off.

Number 4

How can one love be so many persons?
    I see you in a million bodies
      well at least 22
        also you usually have a nice
          bum
        we had great

Number 5

this time 2
lovers
We will catch in a triangle
eachother
you look vulnerable in your bra
and you when I creep up
from behind

Number 6

well I mentioned your number before
I am comfortably afraid of fire
it rises from your shoulder blades
and surrounds your face
your eyes are   huge
and your teeth could cut   metal
how do you keep your lips on your face
they've clearly melted

3 nights 3 knives

The night drew me in I wanted
a companion
on the highway
   realized I had no spare helmet
realized I had no helmet at all
what the hell

This girl came up, grabbed my dick and yanked me around like a
   dog on a leash

The worst part is I don't remember sleeping with this woman
He was French or Italian, definitely Roman
The first knife missed this is not
how the sequence of events went picking it up I had two knives to
   throw
He still advanced
The small one stuck in his chest or his thigh
I retreated
Watching as the large knife that missed me left my hand
It had two blades and no handle
I missed
Retreated to the kitchen where I found the carver
Hid in the darkness by the door,
When he showed
I touched his throat
Dreamed this, not safe.

From Love Bandits: Unite!

Precise landings are not possible for insects.
They bounce off their targets a few times before they settle.
A flower petal; the perfect landing site—
spring-loaded to reduce shock on impact
—a little trampoline.
What a beautiful transaction.

Bees asleep on flowers
In the morning when the air
is too cold
—the canopy of petals closes at dusk
and opens in the morning to let the light in.

Transcendental bumbling machine
life is a pollinating dream
shifts phases from structure to structure
from flower to flower they flutter, they flutter

Camille Came Up
for Diana May Carter

Camille came up from the neighbourhood
the greenlawn treelined
doves for breakfast
walkman on stun
this angel reflected at me in the puddle
held up a burning hoop
and god was bucknaked
as he leapt through it
I found myself
skipping beside her,
yelling to her covered ears.

Attempted Conversion

my ass problem when I was young digging
how girls looked
sitting in the audience, one was up on stage
a troupe of acrobats
and her hair was feathered and she had
rabbit feet dangling from it on leather thongs
earnest concentration, perspiration, buck teeth
sleeveless t-shirt you are accumulating a
score from the time you were born
hippie eyes have dressed me in relics and frocks
down the past five years hit the moment of
decision
the day of judgment
account for yourself boy quiet weak
will you join us?
I thought so
we are in the car he hands me salad
I say oh no
He says oh yes
like a father like a control freak father like a slug of beer in the
shed trying on pink panties like taking pictures of wildflowers like
the old soft man with the sad eyes like a wife stiff never being
plied like driving by schoolyards scoping little boys

For the guy outside the sugar refinery, I smudged your Mandala, you sang me a song by phillip glass.

Read these poems, goofball
I put a lot of work into them
Because of these poems,
My back is extremely sore
Read these poems, goofball,
Lest a person of considerable girth
And murderous nature read them to you
At your funeral I've seen bullet holes
in Hawaiian shirts, they've arrested
a Polynesian in a grass skirt but just barely
the skyline is in jeopardy
and the evidence is mounting
If you want a handbound volume
Call me and I'll make to order.

Tomo Gatche

Gomo Tache
The man is bark
the man is silver bark
bark
bark
the moon is rising
we speak foreign languages
with bad accents
at the base of the mountain
somebody have a cell phone
Excuse me does anybody have a cell phone?
I associate hard liquor with shiny trucks
I associate drinking with driving
I associate smoking with bowling
The dog is on the ground
His belly is near to the ground
He'll eat raw garlic by the clove
Yes the fleas will jump right off his coat
Please give to the Sally Ann
Please give to the Salvation Army
Please give until it hurts under your fingernails
in your eyebrows
The rainbow landed
It crash landed
In a crop circle
where two bodies were making love free
Please turn off the television
Please turn off the fucking television
Light goes for so little these days
Yes a dime bag sure can go a long way

We hike through the forest
Our eyes are slits like squinting
and nomads invented many things
we are all the children of nomads
put down your bag of many things
please put it down and count your blessing(s)
all the houseplants are on fire
and the chimney is full of angry butterflies

Linda
Rogers

Linda **Rogers** has been called the switchboard of
Canadian literature. She sure likes to know what
is going on. Her parents, who needed some phone
time, channelled her compulsion for communication
into writing. They made her get off the blower and go
to university, where she studied classics, theatre, fine
arts and English, ending up with an M.A. in English
Literature. Since then she has mothered, grand-
mothered, made some great bread, taught, performed,
written poetry and prose and children's books, and had
a few moments of glory. She has been awarded the
Stephen Leacock Award, the BC Writer's Poetry Prize,
the Dorothy Livesay Award, the Milton Acorn Award,
the Acorn-Ruckeyser Award, the Voices Israel Prize,
the Cardiff Prize, the Prix Anglais, and the
Confederation Medal for poetry and performance. Her
favourite critic said she "unbuttons language like a
verbal vamp." Rogers and her recycled husband, Rick
van Krugel, live in a yard sale museum and perform
poetry and music together when they are not eating,
shopping, kissing, or shooting pool.

The Dreams of the Rum-soaked Dessert

It's time again and Sunbaby's
laughing over the trees, his great big
head on fire, so everything's cooking,
the coffee, the seeds in the ground,
the old lady next door wearing the red
nightgown she'll hang on the line later,
so everyone in the neighbourhood
will know she got lucky with her bald
husband's sleepy morning erection.

Down the street, a woman with a job
is starting her car. She's running on empty
while her husband sleeps off a drunk
and their kids are up playing house.
They've got their babies sitting in a
line on the sofa, watching cartoons
while they make believe in a tent,
the sheets one of them pissed in
stretched between two kitchen chairs.

Their tent smells like a barn.
"Let's be horses," the girl says.
You be dad and I'll be mum.
She saw them do it once in a dream
about living in the country,
the mare standing there quietly
waiting for him to get down.

Their father is upstairs dreaming
the dreams of the rum-soaked dessert

you light with a match. Last night
he put his hand on the stove, felt
nothing and remembered the time he stumbled
into that bonfire with the baby
fast asleep in his arms. So far, so good.
He was born in the lucky year of the horse.

"Horseshoes up his ass," his mother said.
She was the one who marked every day
on the calendar with a big red
X when her period was late
and ate babas aux rum when her mah-jongg
ladies came for a game, all of them
adding a drop of scotch to their tea,
all of them mothers who counted the fingers
and toes on their children when they were born.
"God, give them ten of everything, please."

*

The man next door was the fireman
who couldn't save my husband when he
went into a fire set by Cossacks
to rescue his mandolin.
But that was another lifetime neither
my husband nor the fireman remembers,
way before the lady with the red nightgown and me,
not sleeping on the roof of our volatile house,
remembering the incarnation when I
sat on the curb chewing tar and watched
Sunbaby rise laughing over the trees.

What is Sunbaby laughing at now,
red leaves on the trees coming down,
red nightgown on the line, red
spots on sheets cherished by bridegrooms,
X's on every calendar rushing to Armageddon,
a young dancer in a cemetery in Valleyview,
Alberta, burying her diseased leg
with a smiling photograph of herself
so it will find her again in heaven,
while her mother, who counted her fingers
and toes the day she was born,
crosses her own and prays.

In fiction, they locked Jane Eyre in a red
room and she went mad trying to remember
the one she left head first, naked and bawling,
the cold air making her breathe and scream,
so that after that girls who read books
began to see the world as red rooms with no
doors and no mothers and bars on the windows
and red lips and scarlet letters the only way out,
every Chinese bride going to her groom
in a red dress and red embroidered slippers,
covering his white painted face with red kisses
while the caged fireflies he's about to give her
tumble frantic, fantastic in the dark.

*

In the beginning, it was dark
before Sunbaby cracked his golden egg
and fell off the fence, before a god

brought us fire on the end of a match,
before Vesuvius burped and covered
Pompeii in ashes, before the bread of
Israelites fleeing seven years of plague
and pestilence could rise, before the Great
Fires of London and San Francisco,
the Japanese city made of paper houses,
and my husband's Latvian village was torched,

before the bombs fell on Hiroshima,
before Doukhobor women stripped
down to their skin and burned their houses
when their children were taken away
and we were taught they were mad, their bodies
bloated by childbirth evidence of that.

*

My mother turned up the volume
and I hid under the table whenever
the midget in her magenta dress
inside the radio sang "Fever," the one
the old lady next door sings every
time she puts on her red nightgown,
just as my mother did, banging her pots
before my father came home from his trials
and doused the fire with a glass of whiskey,
ending the dance of the red shoes,
which I saw at the Varsity theatre
not long after a fire in a theatre
in Montreal caused a stampede
where children were trampled to death

because their mothers and fathers left them,
their red shoes blooming under strangers'
beds while the cowboys in movies shot silver
bullets full of catsup at one another.

This goes on behind closed doors.
I get to see it all from the roof
imagining all the houses with one side
bitten off by a teething infant,
just like the doll's house I've papered
with poems and pictures of children from every
incarnation reduced to ashes by fire,
the old lady next door in her red nightgown,
her husband on top of her, remembering
the sound of the siren, my husband asleep
with his mandolin shaped like a woman beside him
so he doesn't even know I am gone, the drunk
lying on his back, snoring in bed,
a tattoo burned into his hand, his children
sniffing and smelling hay heating up,
their children expressionless,
watching the sun rise on television,
while the young dancer in Valleyview
walks away from her dreams on one leg
and her mother gives up counting.

No wonder Sunbaby's laughing hard.
The world's his cigar, a comic rolled up
and smoked by children, even the horses
playing in their tent, the girl standing there
patiently, on all fours, the boy waiting
for the match to strike, their silent,

expressionless babies lined up on the sofa
waiting for them to discover fire.

Barbara
Colebrook
Peace

Barbara Colebrook Peace was born in northern England, came to Canada as a student, and chose to stay, making this country her home. After completing a master's degree in Classical Literature, she worked for a number of years as an art gallery manager. She is now a freelance editor and poet living in Victoria, British Columbia. Her poetry has been published in such literary journals as the *Malahat Review*, the *Fiddlehead*, *Arc*, and the *Antigonish Review*, as well as in her chapbook *Twelve Silences* (Reference West, 1998) and in the anthology *Threshold: Six Women, Six Poets* (Sono Nis Press, 1998).

THE GENTLE PASSION OF
BARBARA COLEBROOK PEACE

When I experience painting, writing, music, film, or dance, I look for exquisite variations on the one story of human existence. Poetry based on the human struggle to find community engages me most. That was my only bias when I considered emerging poets to introduce in this collection. The ultimate criterion for me is passion: I like to ride on the flow of words and music to a place where I feel madly, truly, deeply; like the woman in the film about grief.

I am grateful for the ironic transparencies of Phyllis Webb, the baroque imagination of Joe Rosenblatt, the passionate idealism of bill bissett, and the musical mysticism of Anne Szumigalski— Canadian poets who took hold of my own intelligence and imagination when I was a younger writer. Now I am listening for the same qualities in those who come after me.

Barbara Colebrook Peace is a transplanted Canadian. The translation from her childhood home in England to this Promised Land in her early adulthood finds an interesting parallel in her writing, which stretches to the unknown, the boundaries of her literate imagination. Barbara, who is married to mathematician Terry Peace, has worked as an art gallery manager and is currently a freelance editor. In her free time, she plays the piano and volunteers with seniors in a nursing home, a source of much of her new poetry. She made her literary debut in *Threshold*, a book introducing new women poets and edited by Rona Murray.

I met Barbara when Diane Morriss suggested I might enjoy working with her as the editor for my poetry book *The Saning* and for *The Broad Canvas*, a collection of portraits of Canadian women artists. Barbara and I soon decided we were "suited opposites." Hers is a quiet passion bred in the gentle, well-laid-out gardens of England, where poetry is a tradition as circumscribed as the ritual for pouring tea. In Barbara's work, I hear the pauses so significant in writing and music, and the humanity essential to writing that transcends the ordinary. True to her last name, her poetry leads us to the peace at the centre.

She sees the downside of that grace as a caution that has kept her out of the fire, a place she considers necessary for creativity. The reserve that I admire so much in her literary watercolours, she considers a barrier to the whole palette for painting. In her more recent poetry dealing with dementia and the marginalized elderly, and particularly in "Gobs," a poem that released a primal flow of memory and desire, she has been stretching toward the wilderness that surrounds her quiet garden. There are many stories waiting there for her to give voice to the voiceless, a preoccupation we share, although we have approached it from different directions.

Poems, we agree, are paintings, some of them abstract and some literal, some ugly in the harsh juxtaposition of colours and some sublime. Barbara is now exploring the rest of the colour wheel. Perhaps, as her metaphorical wild woman, I am her guide— as she is mine to the softer palette of civilization.

Twenty Questions

'Twas brillig, and the slithy toves . . .

—Lewis Carroll, "Jabberwocky"

What is a slithy tove? you ask me
when we meet in the corridor
on the way to poet's corner and the singsong:
a sign you remember who I am,
though my name has drifted like the sun
behind a cloud. Neither of us has a compass,

but we walk more or less north of sorrow
toward the activity room,
the question billowing round you
like a too-big macintosh on a windy day.
I watch you find your way
through the dark intervals in your brain

to a chair beside someone you recognize;
you've told me several times she's
not your wife. You squelch across the room
through rain and wind-blown clouds,
clasping the word *home* so you won't fall.
Everything is just out of your reach:

though you would like to touch
the name and address your father
inked inside every item of stiff
new uniform, satchel, and latin grammar.

Syllable by syllable, we climb
out of your sight
on rungs of invisible riddles,
hic haec hoc over the gym horse,
amo amas amat, returning to a home
that is always more remote.

Now your clothes are labelled for the
laundry, taken and delivered by a stranger.
You stoop over an artificial flower;
doubt falls around you like soot.
What is Saturday afternoon?
Your wife died of cancer. Now there's
a chair, a piano, a woman
you sit beside
in an animal, vegetable, mineral/mourning.

Naked, you dress yourself for the question,
upright in white shirt and navy blazer;
something warm to wear,
as Charles the First on his way to execution:
"Let me have a shirt on more than
ordinary, by reason the season is so sharp
as probably may make me shake . . ."

What is a slithy tove? you ask again
when I've finished reading poems,
Daffodils, The Cremation of Sam McGee,
Lewis Carroll, Edward Lear,
and sit beside you while you drink your tea.
I don't know, I say. *What do you think?*

Maybe you were once
a great flanking buttress of stone,
a lover, a father, a maverick, a moon,
a face that slid round a corner, playing
hide and seek; someone
who made for your children
a shadow rabbit, one long ear pricked
against the dark.

Gobs

Whisht! lads, haad your gobs,
and I'll tell ye aal an aaful story
Whisht! lads, haad your gobs,
and I'll tell ye 'boot the Worm
—"The Lambton Worm," song from northeast England

There are too many people in the world
I'm thinking as I get off the bus
at the corner of Douglas and Yates.
And you're right here, sitting
on the sidewalk, staking your claim
to the niche between trashcan and doorway.
Holes in the knees of your jeans,
rings in ear and nose, your cap
salted with a few quarters. *Spare*
some change for one good joke?

I hurry away without offering
a dime, but you follow me
that night into a dream, standing
just outside my bedroom door
on the upstairs landing of my childhood.
Who are you? I ask, dropping
to the bottom of a shaft. You say
nothing. *What do you have to give me?*
You spit:

       a gob

      *

I swallow, eyes closed, and I'm back:

Shut your gob
    Ha'way man
        Why aye man
Where're ye gangin', hinny?

swirl down back streets and alleys
where we stir fresh tar in the gutter
with lollipop sticks, making treacle
    rainbows

Mrs. Keenan at the kitchen sink
swishing bacon grease from an iron
frying pan, tells me
Miners never wash their backs, pet.
        Mr. Keenan,
back drenched with soot, descends
in a cage to the bottom of the world,
hunkers with a shovel in the pit.
His spine knobbed with scars
scrapes against the ceiling
as he crabs backward on all fours
to his cold tea, bread and bacon dripping.
In a corner, a pit pony, sooty withers,
going blind, sniffs air breathed in and out
a thousand times.
        Far above their heads
Cheviot sheep straggle along Hadrian's Wall,
where slaves of Roman villas once fetched coal,
and soldiers
glinted against the howl of the wind

*

The triangle of grass across the road
is my wilderness.
I clamber over iron railings.
I'm a wild horse, silver brumby,
mane and tail streaming in the wind,
whickering and neighing, hooves pounding

*

Green water at the reservoir
reflects trees and hills, and our uncle
puffing on his pipe. He tells us
it was near here
he and some other village boys
stalked through waist-high heather,
beating grouse for gentlemen to shoot.
A young lord looks down from his horse, asks
Are ye thirsty, lads?
Aye, they mutter, and he answers
Suck on a pebble

*

We play Sardines with our cousins,
cram ourselves in closets,
swish against lavender in wardrobe,
sqeeze down a passageway,
crouch in the cubbyhole, sucking
in our breath, jampacked small as possible

foot against foot
    elbow to elbow
clutching our giggles, sticky
as candy floss,
till there is only one of us seeking—

I always want to be found.
Don't let me be
the only one left in a gobsmacked
speechless world

       * * * * *

We flew over mountains
vast as childhood coming here.
We could see clear back
to the world's spacious beginning:
    earth just risen from the sea
and all doors open

      *

Since you came to me, dream
figure, street person, outcast,
I know I need to eat
the seed words of my first home:
She's a canny bairn . . .

I think of my unborn children
and of the wildflowers
we found sprawling everywhere
along the wooden railroad and down by the river

near my mother's village.
We chose one of each, unwrinkled
their petals,
pressed them under white tissue,
wanting to fix them perfect forever:
cowslip, bluebell, primrose.

*

I walk down Fort Street past
the Dutch Bakery, pies in the window
decorated with gobs of whipped cream.

Buses come and go with gasping doors.
  Are ye thirsty, lads?

Spare some change for one good joke.
You're not here today. What joke
would you have told me?

Something sits unswallowed
like a stone in my mouth. *Gobstoppers,*
we used to call those sweets:
          bulging
                    globes
we moved from cheek to cheek. Wodges
          so huge

we couldn't speak around them.

Epitaph for a Gargoyle

He died before men walked on the moon.

He had a face once; perhaps an old faun
or an eagle
or a sleeping angel, turned
into the shelter of wings. Now
wind and rain have bitten him
down to an eyeless core.
Only his arms are left to glare.

When thawed icicles
drip from the ledge above,
his gouged belly grieves
for someone
      only snow remembers;
grief follows the furrows of his wings,
echoes inside him as a hollow slush.

When he sleeps, illegible
plums appear; night
presses on him star by star,
and scudding clouds
sweep chimneys into darkness—

Then his knees loosen
and fingers slacken; leaving the grass
unmown, the scrabble board paused,
like the rosetta stone, for us to decipher
a word that might be *swort* or *startle*—
How could we know he was our father?

Shadow Icarus

When he was a boy, he spent hours
flat on his stomach on the floor, drawing
cartoons of trucks, remembering not to
crayon over the lines. His mother
moving somewhere about the house—
the passage of the sun across the sky.

Now he lives alone. He looks
for a moment at the rain, stretches
feet to warmth of the heater.
So many years caring for his mother
since his father left; and then her death—

> Again he hears the bang
> against the glass, observes
> the near wing raised, far wing
> stilled, feathers lightly stirring.

He takes from the table
the leather-bound journal *On the Flight
of Birds* he's kept for sixty years.
Writes *sandpiper*, and pauses. Each night
he dreams of stars, water, trees;
a lost limbshadow aches behind his shoulder.
All that he remembers perfect, held
between wind-remembering wings:
his mother's voice calling, and the careful
entries of birds.

j. william

knowles

J. **William Knowles** was born in 1972 in Pasadena, California, to expatriate parents. Since 1981 he has lived in British Columbia, and since 1994 in Victoria. A college graduate in visual art, he has worked as a carpenter's helper, a pizza delivery boy, a dishwasher, a gas jockey, an auto-detailer, a potter's apprentice, a waiter, and a bike courier. His poetry has appeared in *Afterthoughts* and *Libido* (US) and he is currently writing his first novel.

RIDING THE NEW WAVE
WITH J. WILLIAM KNOWLES

Poet Doug Henderson had this pesky neighbour, a bicycle courier who always interrupted his lawn mowing with questions about poetry. Would I take a look at his manuscript? I did and was rewarded with flowers—delivered by bike, of course. Jon Knowles, whose literary designation is J. William to avoid confusion with the author of the adolescent classic *A Separate Peace*, is the answer to a maiden's prayer, a neat freak with manners and a cutting edge the width of a Kevlar mountain bike tire.

Jon—who lives in an antique house with a wood heater and many rooms for the various cubicles of his life: riding, romance, writing, and painting—knows how to paint with words. He gives us moving pictures of his world, the Gen-X fast lane, where everything happens in twenty-four speeds.

Willing to take risks, Jon is pushing the parameters on a childhood constrained by his conservative father, a retired minister and editor of church newsletters—a genre Jon, pedalling for his life, is fleeing in a torrent of words and visual images. When he dares to look back, in risky moments like the one which caused four-minute-miler John Landy to lose the race of his life, we feel what he is leaving.

It is the passionate rush of passing moments that gives his poetry the exhilarating highs a rider experiences at the top of a mountain and on the way down through his personal wilderness, the mean streets he knows with his body. Joy comes from those moments when he and his machine are one and all the pain and poverty he witnesses are left behind.

Knowles is a writer in transition, moving into the century of his maturity. The bicycle is his physical and emotional transportation out of the false paradise of his childhood toward the separate peace promised by his literary namesake. His poems are fresh and their relentless movement is stilled in epiphanous resolutions that betray a mature insight into the meaning of life. Jon is a messenger, literally and figuratively; one of those fallen angels who are willing to crash and burn bringing the good news and the bad to his fellow travellers in lethal last lines.

Jon is such a believer in poetry he actually held a reading at his house to which his fellow couriers were invited. The macho bike dudes laughed when he turned off the techno-industrial music and started to read, but by the end of the first poem, they were listening hard.

Cognitive Dissonance

Grasping for a language
I once knew,
the first thing I find
is my father.
I think of all the things
he forgets, his memory
not precisely fading,
only preoccupied:
an encyclopedia
of Biblical knowledge.

I wish I could hold him
in reverence,
in awe—
funny how he can answer
questions so reasonably
I stop asking,
though a hundred questions
remain.
He calls that
cognitive dissonance.

He's laughably obese,
bald, and badly dressed.
He's been dropping the same
one-liners since 1962.
He's unemployed, living
on the second fat inheritance
of his life.
His father killed himself;

his aunt
died withered,
an incoherent crone
on a morphine-drenched Halloween.

I love him dearly
even though he calls me a pinko
and I can't stand his
right-wing diatribes;
but I can't
take him seriously,
because with the weather
the way it has been,
and things heating up
in China,
I'm terrified
that he might be right
about something.

Chopping Wood:

the heft of the old axe, the warmth
expanding through your chest
with every blow, all the testosterone
rising to your head. You think,
this is what it is to be a man:
the violence of this act.

You imagine yourself a Viking,
cleaving the skulls of villagers
on the shores of Brittany,
providing for the blond wife
and children you left on the other side
of a drakkar-travelled channel.

Here in the 20th century, you think
of the girl you're dating, how
she said she'd love to have a house,
how fun it would be to have a garden;
you wonder how she'd feel
if she saw you now,
swinging this big axe. Do you
fit into her vision?
Despite the house, the garden,
and this act, you feel
like a boy, thinking this way.

It takes a long time
to reduce this knotty log
to kindling, and
it burns so quickly

in the stove that
warms your house.
It took a lot longer
for the tree to grow.
This is what it is
to be human,
to reduce in an hour
what took a century
to rise up.

Broken Day

As a teenager
I wanted to be a martyr,
burn at some stake,
hang on some cross, maybe.
Now,
though I've broken bones,
and bled profusely on occasion,
I want to die
when I have a hangover,
swearing I'll never drink again.

Sitting here, heartsick,
(this is almost a comfort zone)
I think of a frog's
dead legs
twitching at the touch of electrodes
in a high-school science class
and I beg the silence
for a stimulus.

But the phone
doesn't ring all day
and I sit here, paralyzed,
nothing getting done,
ecologies growing
in the laundry basket
and the bathroom.

I want to be
one of those mangy crows

picking at the garbage
under the tables of sidewalk cafés;
a simple life:
fear, hunger, fights
with seagulls and rival males . . .
well, maybe not so simple,
not even much different.

Maybe a dog:
all that language thrown at you
because you lay down
on the wrong soft spot,
because you chewed up something,
not knowing why.

Forget dogs.

When I stare at the stormy sea,
or the frothy boil
of a fast-running river,
it never occurs to me
that place is cold,
that I can't breathe there,
I just want to throw myself in.

Untitled No. 23

The language you speak
comes easily to me now.
You have the
unrelenting stare
of a true-hearted masochist,
hurt me, hurt me . . .
or I'll hurt you.
There is no
in-between.

I think of all the games
we could play
if I were a crueller man,
if I could crack my tongue
like a whip, unfettered
by the cool tether of guilt,
but I always come around
to that quaint old yearning.
I know I would just
fall in love with you,
and that's where it all falls apart,
where the children get up
and abandon the game,
the last little kid
throwing the board
and all the little pieces
into the air.

Dirty Streets

It's like some chemical
trips in my brain when
I open the doors of City Hall
to the screaming
of a yellow fire truck
and sidewalks adrift
in pink blossoms
and cigarette butts.

The chaos of traffic
and street people
and the wet spring wind
wash over me
like only real life can,
and I can't wait
to unlock my bike
and throw myself
into the mess.

For several blocks
I draft a tour bus,
my feet floating
with the pedals,
the speed effortless,
watching and listening
to the brake lights
and the pitch of the engine
like my life depends on it—
because it does.

I look away from the brake lights
to see the blur of buildings,
pedestrians, and parked cars
and hope there's no cop
in the audience.

I drop at the police station
and for a moment lament
the lack of real crime
in this city of tourists
as I watch the cops
greet all comers
to the inquiries counter
with the cheerful deference
of retail clerks.

On the way out I get tangled
with my bike, my radio cord
hooked behind the seat,
and some super-suave
black man tells me
I'm held prisoner to myself
and I think If only you knew.

One of my mates, fired last week,
has traded his Styrofoam helmet
for a suede fedora
and now he's busking
on the sidewalk,
messenger of the blues,

singing with the conviction
of the newly underemployed,
he and I now worlds apart,
still working the same dirty streets.

Her Politics

If I think about it long enough
I can
make her clothes fall off,

each item dropping
in a languid spiral
to the floor,

a museum of modesty,
her dress, her underthings:
the exhibition of the century;

her nakedness the
once-in-history event commemorated
on the dusty Smithsonian floor.

Like Miller's Germaine, her vagina
something omnimagnificent,
the eighth wonder of the world,

her breasts advancing across the room:
a couple of
intercontinental ballistic missiles,

the bane and delight
of the Persian empire,
the death of so many

frustrated soldiers masturbating
with their AK-47s and Kalishnikovs
from Baghdad to Belgrade.

Feathered Corpse

In the morning I take the pill
that keeps me a little more alive,
all those minerals on my tongue
never meant to be tasted,
and I open the door
to leering Christian faces,
the Lord's Little Lambs
in adolescent moustaches
and Wal-Mart finery.

The door not quite slammed,
I almost kneel in prayer,
my soul a distended bowel,
and then I remember
the half-mad, wholly
beautiful Indian woman
hoping for a coffee-date
and I think of Suzanne's
tea and oranges and stay erect
a little longer to streak
through the constant traffic
in tights and racing stripes,
looking like a crew-cut
Star Wars disco faggot
following the religious discourse
of fish and amphibians
on trunk lids and tailgates.

A wailing ambulance passes me,
and I ride over a dead bird
pancaked on the pavement
and I think This is fun!
but this is not the life
I want to live, not
the death I want to die,
a forgotten warless soldier,
a feathered corpse in the city street,
something less, even,
than chisel marks on marble.

The Best Kind of Fear

Narrow winding
rock-bitten track:
the SPRONG of the suspension fork
topping out, the back wheel
slides sideways on wet root,
the inner ear compensates
like some pure instinct;
single-minded,
you are two fat tires,
dirt,
mud,
the blur of trees.

The climb:
teeth together,
snarling the air
into your lungs,
rubber sinks into dirt,
claws at rock;
exertion, an acid,
floods your muscles;
then the top:
a saving splash of water
from the bottle.

The descent:
lean back, you are
weightless with adrenaline,
eyes wide
with the best kind of fear,
bump,
bounce,
slide;
you can't turn back now,
can't re-think,
don't hesitate
or you will lose your line,
break an arm,
break a collar bone,
or break your neck;
just lean back
and don't brake too hard—
now you're alive.

Vera Wabegijig is Anishnawbe:kwe, from
Mississauga First Nation, Ontario, a member
of the Bear Clan. Because she is a bear who doesn't
sleep during winter, she has packed quite a bit of
experience into her young life. An activist for her
people, this graduate of the En'owkin International
School of Writing has been gathering credentials,
including Canada Council and Cultural Services
Awards, the William Armstrong Literary Award, and
several publishing credits. The mother of a young
daughter, she is currently working on a degree in
Creative Writing at the University of British
Columbia, where her energy, integrity, and sense of
humour mark her as a writer to watch. She hopes to
give her idol, Thomas King, a run for his money and
promises to remember her mentor, Linda Rogers,
when she is "semi-famous."

THE NEW VERSION ACCORDING TO VERA WABEGIJIG

My mother once came back from New York, where she had seen performances of *A Man for All Seasons* in which Anthony Quinn and Sir Lawrence Olivier exchanged the lead roles. It was so real from her front row seat. "They spat on me!" she reported. You could call it a baptism as the holy shower rained down. This is what I expect from poetry, to feel blessed and transformed by the experience.

Ironic humanity is the underpainting in the poetry of Vera Wabegijig, an Anishnawbe:kwe from Mississauga First Nation, Ontario. She presents in plain modern language the ethic of an ancient and benign culture whose only desideratum was harmony with the universe. The transformations in poetry are also the mechanics of her culture, which sees man, animal, and nature morphing one into the other. Because these rhythms have been disturbed by the Whitecomers and the ages of science and the new unreason of Voltaire's Bastards, she is a metaphorical canary in the coal mine, scolding us, in a radiant flow of words, to fresh awakenings.

This canary is one incarnation of the Trickster, Raven or Coyote, taking on whatever voice is needed to provide contemporary cautionary tales. Her poems, although framed in the architecture of a storytelling civilization, have the freshness of immediacy, because her mythology is flexible in the moment.

Vera was my student in creative writing at the University of Victoria. In a year blessed with amazing young poets, she made me choose her for the opposite reasons I was drawn to Barbara Colebrook Peace. A whole generation younger than myself, Vera has already been deep in the woods, revisiting the steps of her ancestress, Wild Woman.

Vera has lived with the voiceless. Like the transformation masks of her culture, she has changed her shape and wrestled a path through the forest to a clearing where her stories have access to light. As an aboriginal woman, she has experienced all the historical prerogatives of modern First Nations people, some of them soul building and some soul destroying. She carries this information into the modern world, where her powerful developing voice reaches for every octave from past to present.

Story is the matrix of her culture and her use of it is powerful. Although her experiences are contemporary and her wilderness cross-hatched by urban streets, where gods and monsters reconform with every satanic invention, her story structure is timeless. She has the sense of humour that is the gift of adversity, and the rage that goes with it. Her passion is a love of her oral culture and the will to make it accessible to others so that they might understand.

The single mother of a young daughter, appropriately named Storm, Vera has already distinguished herself as a spokeswoman of her generation and her people. She hopes her journey will take her to undiscovered worlds. It can't help but take us all to a better place. After all, she says in "creation story," "in the beginning there was darkness . . . how else do you start a story?" We are presented with a humorous inversion of Genesis—a new version for our time.

sweat lodge in downtown toronto

delia drags her coppertone body down dundas,
and tracks through an alley over to spadina,
a dumpster diver offers her rice wine & moldy pizza,
the way a priest offers holy eucharist,
'cept for this prayer slips between a broken tooth
and a heavy bottom lip

sta-gots! delia shakes her head, body like a wet dog drying off,
maybe some other time i'll break bread with you
and drink your holy blood

delia scans a poster ad: "Summer Solstice Feast"
or was it "National Aboriginal Day"?
down at the local skin hang-out,
you know, the friendship centre
it doesn't really matter to delia
after all, a feast is a feast, and free food
is good food

fry bread, venison, three sister soup
guides her like a vision quest
through the sizzling toronto smog,
or a first time sweat at dreamer's rock
only **all my relations** doesn't work
and she is still not home,
with the air conditioner's icy blasts

after seconds of fry bread & blueberry jam
and a sixth cup of red rose tea,
eagleheart, the city rez drum group,

begin a two-stepper frenzy
a sweaty, slighty-brown stag reaches for delia's hand,
chh, in her cree-way, not even,
it's hotter than a bowl of sex
and i am ass deep in venison already.
chhh! sssss! ehhhn!
all neechees exclaim in unison
and delia goes breasts first into his skinny arms

dusk settles in for a nightcap
while delia & her new/used buck walk away,
hands in each other's back pocket
and the door of the sweat lodge
in downtown toronto
swings shut to rez-urbia for the night.

Glossary
sta-gots—Cree slang ("Get out of here")
all my relations—if a sweat is heating up, say this, fast
neechees—other skins

big brown beautiful bannock stuffed indians

sit in smoke-filled bingo halls
offer silent prayers to bingo god
as dabbing number to win money
to return every night
for the gamble stomp
instead of
feeding hungry cubs
who inhale solvents and faint
in abandoned school yards

beautiful bannock stuffed indians
fuck each other on friday nights
one indian man
fathers thirteen offspring
from seven wives
they all hate him
'cept for one little boy
who loves his daddy
and scribbles, i miss you,
with broken crayons,
when you coming home?

bannock stuffed indians
keep warm around fire
under train bridge
that reeks of urine
listerine bottles circle
winos with fresh breath
and crippled limbs
as i sit at home

eating stale bannock
with lard, and witness
re-runs of North of 60

wild

blueberry fields in mid-august waited patiently   their plump blue bodies
hang from bent twigs   exhaling a sweet blue fragment   which i inhale
deeply as i reach down slowly to pick one and squeeze it into my mouth   i
continue to pick a few more not hesitating to indulge in this berry eating
frenzy   until i hear my granny yelling in the distance, you better quit
eating all the berries

i let my eyes burn into my little cousin natalie   there she is stuffing
all her blueberries into her mork & mindy t-shirt squashing them all and
sucking out all its juice through her now blue stained shirt and granny
smiles her toothless smile   i don't blame her   those berries are just so
good, so ripe, so perfect   on a hot day like today

i wander away from my cousins to a secluded area where there is an abundance
of berries and i flop unto the moss covered earth   sky is a crisp blue
and sun waltzes above me   some sultry dance i must say   i look around and
i am tangled up in blue

i pick a berry, set it into my empty basket, plop, then another, plop, then
another, plop, plop, plop   the basket quickly fills   only five more to
go it becomes a competition, this berry picking business   who picks the
most, in the least amount of time   by the time i was eight i was a pro
you get into this rhythm, you switch to automatic until a horsefly lands
in the middle of your back   ouch those little pricks   and you can't stop
from scratching where the assault occurred

i untangle myself from the blueberries and head back to where the family
is, but i am dizzy from this picking escapade   and sun soaked right into
me   causing my inner compass to point north in every direction   i call
out, only my echo answers, face it you're lost

i sit back down in the bare naked berry patch, distressed, i listen real
hard, only bugs and grasshoppers sing me the blues   i close my eyes   if
only, i could click my moccasins together three times   i wanna go home, i
wanna go home, only when i open my eyes i am not surrounded by a scarecrow,
lion or a tin man   just my granny slouched over touching my head   she
has a small bottle of holy oil, she dabs her fingers, and begins to bless me,
putting the sign of the cross on my forehead

i sit up quickly which startles my old granny, granny you could've used
blueberry juice   granny laughs, i should've, you'd have a blue cross stain
in the middle of your small brown forehead, and then what the heck would
that signify?   i shrug my shoulders   i notice my little cousin
natalie, i call her, natalie, natalie come here, i want to bless you
she spins around like a dragonfly, she don't care, she's already a
tie-dyed blueberry baby picking indian

slang tongue twist

brand extension on the rez:
hilfiger, adidas, nike, klein
hang loose on brown bodies,
from hats to pants even cool undies.

walking billboards is the latest trend
on our littered pow-wow grounds,
there's not enough long braids that dangle
or mother tongue words that tangle

skins dance,
but not to the pow-wow drum.
it's a hip-hop beat from ghetto streets.
here they break dance, a funky horse prance,
flip high fives and slam each other's mothers
and lay the beats to their blood brothers

brand extension reaches
bush rez and rezurbia,
a disillusion of community
where skin is against skin
in a neo-warrior gang clash

chicken bone

hands clutch
around throat
grasp
for air

a chicken
bone
stuck

too hungry
after days
starving

forget
how to chew
just swallow

arms wrap
around stomach
from behind
jerks me up

chicken bone
flies across
the room
and lands in
garbage can.

creation story

number one

in the beginning there was darkness . . . how else do you start a story?   the
indian agent came to the rez today, without permission, without a
reservation   i asked that indian agent, can i get assimilated with a
shake of colonization?   that indian agent thought i was joking, i was damn
serious   what indian doesn't want the ideology of good christian
(im)morals   what indian wants their mother (tongue)   so that indian
agent gave me a treaty   gave me a nice hudson's bay blanket too   both
gifts filled with lies and dis(ease)   maybe that indian agent didn't
understand my sarcasm   maybe that indian agent saw into the future . . .

number two

my best friend isn't a dog   my best friend is coyote, who told me a
creation story: in the beginning there was no darkness, no darkness, just
coyote . . . and a few of coyote's mates (of course): raven, nanabush,
wesakejack, glooscap, spider . . .   well you get the picture, a world full of
tricksters, which equals a world of chaos   this is where we come in, us
humans . . .   coyote was bored, and you can imagine, so were the others, they
needed some conflict, like a real good creation story . . .   so the
tricksters gathered together one boring day and collected lint from their
pockets and made us real   of course, they put us all in the wrong places
on this turtle shaped island, so we had to migrate to where the terrain was
just right   'cause we all know there's no such thing as a land bridge . . .

number three

so there was darkness in all of us   so coyote was smart this time and gave
us flashlights   but at this time we didn't know how to use our thumbs

so nanabush gave us fire   but the trickster council didn't mention
anything about responsibility, so humans destroyed themselves again
wesakejack dug for more lint and suggested, first responsibility then fire
  humans evolved quickly when learned how to use their fifth digit, their
thumbs, and they began to make wheels, clubs and bows & arrows   at this
time, they discovered a rising urge to fight over food, territory and
copulation rights . . .

storm

my daughter's body slides from between my legs,
a butterfly shaking loose from its cocoon.

her father holds a braid of sweetgrass as it slowly burns,
and our nurse passes this tiny brown body,
all legs, arms and black furry hair,
not a single cry escapes from her
just curious eyes that dart around
then settle into mine.

Patricia Young's collection *More Watery Still* was nominated for the Governor General's Award in 1994. She has also won the Pat Lowther Memorial Award, the Dorothy Livesay Prize for poetry, the League of Canadian Poets' National Poetry Competition, and the *National Magazine* Award for Poetry. In 1999 she served as the first Ralph Gustafson Poet-in-Residence at Malaspina University College in Nanaimo. A collection of her new and selected poems, *Ruin and Beauty*, will be published in 2000 by House of Anansi. Patricia Young lives in Victoria, British Columbia, with her husband and two children.

Chalk Eater

Once the fourth-largest lake in the world, the [Aral] sea
has been . . . strangled by a massive diversion of water to
irrigate the vast cotton fields of Central Asia. —Globe and Mail

Sometimes I dream I'm a windswept boy wandering the towns
of northern Uzbekistan eating my own clothes.

That my mother, up to her knees in muddy seabed,
is a crude statue carved out of chalk.
The desire to eat her is strong in me.

My sister drags herself through pools of stagnant
water searching for a chunk of clay.

Dust blows across our faces,
the stink of pesticides burns our skin.

I remember a blueberry bush, a yellow bird
caught in its branches but what can a sea remember—
a stomach full of trout?

Sewage leaks through the earth like sludge in an old man's veins.

In the distance my father is leaning over his boat, pulling in nets.
This must be Muynak before he died of TB
and the hulks of rotting trollers pocked the desert.

Each autumn, the body I was born with
shakes its fist at the fields of cotton.
And still the women pick through the night,

clouds forming above the terrible harvest.

What now, now the children have limped away
in their half-eaten shirts and the Amu Darya ends in
   a toxic trickle?

If I follow the ancient river will I find
a pine grove, deer grazing on nasturtiums?

Once, my father told me the stars were dew in heaven
but when he spread his fingers
misshapen minnows
spilled from his hands
as though from a dead girl's belly.

Camp-out

We don't know where we're going, just that we're following our father through the light and shadow of the northern wilderness. The evening air blows soft against our faces. Somewhere our mother is strapped down in a hospital bed. Up to our chests, we push through salal until suddenly, as though at a crosswalk, our father holds out his arm. He points to the dump in the clearing: bears and their cubs foraging through mountains of garbage.

We start walking and I notice my older sister Mary is hunched like an old woman, a bag of potatoes over her shoulder. Every few minutes, the younger one, Jane, sits in the dirt to pull twigs and leaves from her sweater and hair.

In how many picture books have we seen cedar trees like this one—hollowed out with windows and stairs and lanterns of welcome. Hanging from a branch is a sign that says *110 Mile House*. There is nothing to do but wait on the porch steps for our father to drink his beer. It's dark when cigarette smoke wafts out the inn's door. One at a time the stars blink on.

I want, Jane whimpers, following our father through the forest. This time we stop at a hardware store into which he disappears, emerging moments later with an Eskimo doll dressed in snow pants and a little blue parka. Real fox fur frames the hood. Jane grabs the doll. I kick the back of Mary's ankles, making her spill the bag of potatoes. On hands and knees, we grope the earth. *How old are you, what's your favourite colour, next year can I blow out your birthday candles?* I ask, but Mary refuses to answer.

By now our mother's given birth to a five-pound infant we'll call *Baby* for years. *Stupid potatoes*, Mary hisses at our father who promises one day to take her to a hockey game in a southern city. Hotdogs, buttered corn, the sweat of men.

We stop near a stream and set up camp for the night. At six years old I love the canvas smell of a tent as much as I love anything. *Lucy*, Jane murmurs, rocking her doll by the fire, pinching its plastic cheeks. That night I dream Baby's head floats on a lily pad, her hair a burning mop.

The next morning our father wakes to the song of a hooded oriole. Beside him, one sleeping bag's empty. He inflates, becomes huge as Paul Bunyan leaping over thousand-year-old fir trees as though they were blades of grass. There's the sound of rushing water. Mary or Jane? You guess who's down by the river turning into a stone.

Fallen Angel

And it came to pass, when men began to multiply on the
face of the earth, and daughters were born unto them, that
the sons of God saw the daughters of men that they were fair;
and they took them wives of all which they chose.

—Genesis 6:1-2

I walked a long way in an old pair of sandals
and when I looked up I saw the fiery
shape of a man revolving on itself
in a field of blue space.
My knees locked, my tongue broke like a flame.

In those days the world was immaculate
and devoid of memory. It was difficult to think
without hearing the gold language of birds.

His face emerged slowly, feature by nascent feature.
And then his neck/chest/thighs.
In this way he put on a body of flesh
as though putting on a suit of fine cloth.

Crocuses bloomed over the dip of thorny hills
and for a moment my eye cocked toward Paradise.

Braiding the horse's mane
I'd feel him lean into the blank
pools at the edge of my thoughts, he was clean
intelligence, the tongue falling on my skin
fantastic as a weapon.

Or grinding corn, the upperstone between us,
I had only to look in his eyes and I was
pulled upwards, the passion of that strange god
did with me as it pleased, I no longer knew
what I was—woman or jackal, fish or flying thing.

I didn't care where he'd come from nor did I ask
if he'd been sent to me as some kind of balm
to the awful wound of being human.

Only once before he left through the garden gate
did he speak of the place he'd forsaken,
his words engorged with regret,
the same swollen sounds
scratched on the walls outside Eden.

And then the gibberish in his sleep—
the sky splitting open like a goat-skin bottle,
wooden doors slamming shut.

Those final days of disquiet—walking beneath the aloe tree,
its leaves trembling like the senses. Everything
from the protozoan to our hybrid son
banging his breakfast bowl
appeared resplendent and tragic.

My sight reached beyond the unscrubbed table.
I saw that even the lowest embryo
manifests will, desire, a terrible cunning.
Who could I blame when the rains finally fell
and he passed through my world
like the voice of an animal?

Samara brock

Samara Brock grew up on a vineyard in the small town of Okanagan Falls, British Columbia. She has lived in Victoria for the past eight years, minus brief stints in Vancouver, Cortes Island, New York, and Seoul. She graduated from the University of Victoria in 1998 with a degree in History and Environmental Studies. Samara currently works at LifeCycles, a non-profit organization in Victoria that focuses on issues of food security and urban sustainability. Though she has no musical ability she hopes to one day become an opera singer.

TADPOLES AND BEES:
POETRY BORN OF THE NATURAL WORLD

Samara Brock works close to the earth. She rides her bicycle everywhere and her hands are often digging in the dirt. In the past year she has also begun to write lovely, evocative poems.

Samara's fascination with words goes back to childhood, when she wrote in a journal. She has always been intrigued by the way words fall on a page, the way they can be arranged and rearranged, turned on their heads, fit together like a Rubik's cube. At university she had close friends who wrote poetry and with them she attended many public readings, but it wasn't until Samara finally gave herself permission to create without judging that she began to write her own poems.

In her third year of university, Samara took a break and moved to Cortes Island to participate in an eight-month organic gardening course. When she returned to university she had a mission: to help establish a community garden on campus for students who, because they lived in apartments or basement suites, did not have access to land. With a group of other committed volunteers she lobbied for a year and a half, and finally the university allotted a plot of land near the McKinnon Gym for the garden project. Two years later this space is still being used by members of the university community to grow organic fruits and vegetables.

Samara's connection to the natural world and her passionate interest in the "survival of small things" inform her writing. Reading her poems, we are brought up close to tadpoles, ladybug wings, bees. In the poems where she returns to childhood, this vision is magnified. We see the "small things" through the eyes of a child, and the world is suddenly beautifully dream-like and fraught with danger at the same time.

These poems are palpable; they have texture. At the same time, their delicate, assured imagery creates an atmosphere that is both real and surreal. In "Something Dust Covered," the stillness and heat of a hot summer day are so vividly described we can taste the dirt in our teeth. This is what we long for in poetry: to feel the exquisitely crafted words lift us out of ourselves and carry us into other realities, where we might suddenly find ourselves swimming through the long evening in a "buried home / dug into the hillside."

Bee Space

Though the followers of Pythagoras lived on a diet
of bread and honey, it wasn't until 1851 that apiarist
Lorenzo Lorraine Langstroth came up with the
concept of *bee space.*

The loneliest I have ever been was in Seoul, Korea. It
was my twenty-fifth birthday. I sat in the teachers'
dorm staring out the bars on the window. The empty
hum of cicadas clung to every surface, expanding the
hollow of the tiny, humid room.

*bee space: the dimension of three-eighths of an inch needed
between all parts of the hive to ensure free movement of the bee.*

The first time you almost spent the night I looked
out the window after you and the shadows of trees
were playing the neighbours' white picket fence like
piano keys.

That's a lie, I hadn't even seen you that day. It was
still spring and windy outside. We barely knew one
another. I looked out the window to check if the
white plastic bag still hung like some disguise for
insect life from the cherry tree. It had been sus-
pended there since we first met.

There are 88 keys on the piano. 36 black ones, 52
white. The black ones are sad, the white ones less so.
Though my hands have moved over all 88, they have
never strung them together into music.

It's summer now and you sit playing the piano in my living room. The builder of the piano must have known the concept of bee space. Known that notes, like bees, can get trapped inside the hollow if measurements aren't right. Now, instead, they move around the room filling it with their sweet hum.

Prone

When she was young
she wandered off for hours,
came back way past bedtime,
ate reheated scrambled eggs.
Not sure whether they had looked for her
or not. Wouldn't have mattered anyways
she went so far,
and she wouldn't have known her name
even if they had called it.

They never used her name.
Not even the time her dad
and a seven-foot veterinarian
were playing tennis and the giant vet
served a ball right into her nose.
Her mother brought a cold washcloth
down from the house.
The game went on.
She wasn't a horse.
It was only a nosebleed.

The first time she realized she had a name
was when she received *The Junior Book of First Aid*.
Inside the cover was a sticker of a dragon
with the words—*This Book Belongs To:* ....
She was disappointed, had imagined
a head-against-the-diving-board name
like *Gertrude*.

The accidents didn't stop after that though.
A year later she was walking a small dog
when she broke her arm.
She's still not quite sure of the details.
The leash must have acted as a lever
and for a split second she was a part
of an ancient machine.

Survival of Small Things

In the bug-heavy heat
of summer my family moves
to Nana's house:
by the lake, secure
in the concave of its own valley,
ringed with willow.

Sun and shadow move
over each other here
like playmates,
smooth leaves
coupling in the wind.

Under the blue overhang of branch
on water, the quiet collects
tiny black whales.
My hands push mason jars
through water
to gather a tadpole mass.

Across from me, my brother,
belly down on diving board.
The smell of wet bread
he uses to catch minnows
for Bingo, Nana's grey cat.
The crack of snapping spines
over hot concrete.

Inside the peeling orange
of 108 Jade Bay,

we keep a rooster.
Past the drapings of Nana's wool:
violet, indigo, rose.
Past the ammonia-soaked air
of home-made dyes,
next to the furnace.

Injured by mink, the rooster
cowers in a cardboard box.
Our mother shows us how to feed.
Never by hand.

At night the crickets send the air
cooling with their song.
Tucked into the cotton
of Nana's bed I dream
the survival of small things;
jarred whales, one-legged rooster,
quick flashes of light
escaping the net.

Something Dust Covered

In our town, dust rushed
into the vacuum of noon's electric heat,
pushed its way into the concrete cracks
of Main Street, insulated the neon hum
of the fast food restaurant,
etched its black lines into summer's shoeless feet.

These lines mapped our days.
Fine-netted wings carried my friends and me
through dust-thick air.
From the sun-starched tin of their trailers
to the bell-less hollow of the schoolyard.

Come evening, their fathers returned
home from the mill.
Fading light swallowed our games,
wings folded behind backs.
Inside, another landscape
was shaped by fathers'
rough hands.

Each night, mother came down
from our farm above.
Picked up my brother and me,
wiped the dust from our skin, carried us
back to the cool brick of our buried home,
dug into the hillside.

In this underground,
we swam through our evenings,

coming up from the water
only to be dried off and put to bed.

Summers passed.
We all grew our way out of hand-me-downs,
bellies pushing shirts from shorts.
But mother's nightly rescue marked
my brother and me
like the line where a water drop
has moved over something
covered in dust.

Roommate

Spring lightning purifies air green.
I am offered a new home.
The storm, like potter's hands,
shapes decision from inside.

Walking home she helps me
to catch my first firefly.
Slow in the cool night,
its abdomen shines against our fingers.

In summer she moves the table outside,
places new flowers at every meal.
In the evening we sit on the balcony,
listen to jazz from the college station,
take pictures of our white toes
and glasses propped on the edge of the railing.
She tells me we are in love.

Tiny lizards crawl from between the shingles,
grow fat in the August sun.
I stay where I am.

Cold touches leaf tips red,
letters begin to arrive for her.
She hides them,
but not before I see
they contain celebrations of her.
Portraits from all angles
done by some stranger's hand.

Odd wet hatchings
come to the house in October.
Albino fruit flies
and black beetles as thick as thumbs.

I keep to my room.
Feel I have been collected
like the wasp nest, insects from the sill
which she saves to make into paper.
I tunnel past her
through cold, thin walls.

On the first warm day
tiny moths rise from between
the tiles of the balcony.
Grey like brick.
A mosaic taking to air.

When I pack to leave
she isn't surprised.
Gives me pieces of things:
ladybug wings, a bowl shard.

Vision of God

I don't remember it,
but Laura must have one day arrived
at the old house at the bottom
of the hill with its wasp-paper walls
and cat-sweet smell.

She must have known
from the start I'd be willing,
grabbing my hand to show me
how to carry the awkward weight
of kittens by their tails.

How to wander for hours from home,
down to the vineyards.
Holler our five-year-old insults
at pickers, hurl grapes at dogs
until the white of them
stained red.

How to get to the biggest ponderosa,
play her games:
Chinese, Japanese
Dirty knees
Look at these!

Until I lay awake confessing
to something in the dark:
Bell-bottomed, moustached
like Denis
the town's dump truck driver.

Mother taught me to kneel
beside my bed.
Ask for lives of the injured
farm animals.

I began to save spiders to put outside,
buried favourite toys
(rainbow harmonica, miniature glass giraffe)
refused to play with Laura
when boys followed her
into the bushes behind the portable.

I don't remember it,
but she must have one day left
the old house at the bottom
of the hill with its slamming screen doors.

Before the demolition began
and all that remained
was the porcelain shape of a toilet
among those crumbling walls.

Marlene Grand Maitre

Marlene Grand Maitre was born in Vancouver and grew up in northwestern Ontario. After graduating with degrees in French Literature and Library Science, she worked in college and university libraries. She has recently returned to that environment after many years as coordinator of a support program for abused women involved with the justice system, and as a transition house counsellor. Marlene was also a trainer of transition house workers, a counsellor in a treatment program for abusive men, and an employment counsellor. She has been writing poetry for three years, and was chosen as a delegate to the BC Festival of the Arts in May 1999.

STRAIGHT TO THE HEART OF THINGS

Marlene Grand Maitre began to write poetry three years ago. In fact, she can remember the day she wrote her first poem. When she looks back she realizes that writing that poem opened a door—a door into a world where it was possible to grapple with the chaos of experience, and then craft that experience into something beautiful.

In February 1997, Marlene was employed as a counsellor in an employment training program and was beginning to feel worn down by the pressures of the job. Despite this, or perhaps because of it, she began to feel a compulsion to write. *What* she wanted to write she didn't know. Even so, she plunged right in, signing up for an eight-week evening writing course offered through the University of Victoria's Continuing Education Department. Each week Marlene wrote unstructured prose in response to the exercises assigned by her instructor, Cherie Thiessen, to whom Marlene gives credit for encouraging her at the beginning. By the end of the course, Marlene was surprised and delighted to find herself shaping her words into a poem.

When Marlene speaks of her excitement about and love of poetry, she also expresses a deep sadness: that she came to it in her early fifties; that she has so much to learn and not enough time to learn it. And yet when I read her poems, I do not feel as though I'm reading the work of a novice. These poems have arrived after years of living.

Without equivocation, Marlene asks the animals in "The Lost Herd" why they have come to her when she is "in mid-life / and childless." Perhaps, these "animals" are poems; perhaps, they have come to Marlene now, nudging her "belly with their hooves," because they can no longer wait to be written. There is an urgency to Marlene's words, a need to write about the game a father plays with a child in an upstairs room, or the curses a grandmother shouts at her dead husband.

While it may take a young writer many years to find her voice, it seems to me Marlene's "voice" was fully formed when she began to write three years ago. Whether dealing with issues around childhood, marriage, abuse, or aging, Marlene's poems go straight to the heart of things. Her clean, spare writing speaks with a searing beauty.

Blood Pancakes at the Hoito

The Duluth bus depot, a place for endings
like the last holiday mother and I take
before she remarries.
At the curved lunch counter, I spin on a stool,
pick at the crusts of my Stan & Sy.
Les Paul and Mary Ford sing "Vaya con Dios"
on the chrome and candy apple jukebox.

My new father, hung over
after another three-day poker game,
will later sit alone
and eat blood pancakes at the Hoito,
listen to the Red Finns and the White Finns
arguing about Communism in his first language,
one that calls a cold wind
stepmother's breath.

Under a Fierce Sun

Imagine you are a young giraffe
under a fierce sun, your mother's body
makes a pool of shade for you until
it is safe to come out. Imagine this
while you wait under a bush in the garden
for your mother to find her body,
place it between you and the world,
pressing against your smallness.
Where is your mother?
In the bathroom she searches the mirror,
stroking her reflection.
In the bedroom she rubs the hollow
next to your sleeping father.
Opens your toy box on the porch, uncovers
her broken doll, its porcelain head,
eyes wide open and frozen
as if they see her at your age, hiding
under her father's house.

My Mother at 80,

is slowly going blind.
She sits at her kitchen table
listening to the voice in her clock
announce the hour, struggles
to describe the quality
of her sadness—not the white
of bones bleached by sunlight
but the white of thin roots
reaching for darkness.

Taxi Back to 1950

Take Oikonen's Taxi back to 1950;
the driver will know the way to
129 Prospect Avenue. Press your nose
to the living room window, watch me
dance in a rummage sale nightgown
and satin bed jacket, Big Band music
rising from the soles of my feet:
Glenn Miller, the Dorsey Brothers.
Mother perches on the edge
of the horsehair sofa, dressed
in her green taffeta that sounds
like a party when she moves.
Beer and Evening in Paris.
Don't be frightened by the noise
coming from the basement.
It's just Grandma stoking the furnace,
her hair bursting into flames.
Hands on hips, she stands
in front of my dead grandfather's closet,
cursing: *Eames, you bastard,*
leaving me to shovel all this coal.
He rides out in his Masonic apron
on King Billy's white horse,
rounds up Catholics to torture
in the vises on his workbench.
Later I will fall asleep listening
to his enemies howl below.
My grandmother, fiery
halo lighting the way,
will lead him back to the closet.

Rorschach

At twelve, the iron scent and your first bloodstains
bring a flood of earlier shapes:
Aunt Minnie in her corner of the kitchen
near the slops, skinning tomatoes for soup.
Mother at her piano in the parlour
slipping between the black and white keys,
the "Spring Violets" in her song
washing the house in fresh purple.
Father upstairs with you,
playing a game: he takes
your pyjama bottoms,
ties them to the bedpost,
a pirate flag. You take him
in your hand, then your mouth; he marks you
with his pungent smell. You shrink,
curl up tight inside the metronome
on mother's piano, the pendulum
keeping time, keeping time.

Breaking the Surface

All summer the adults drank
rye and coke on the cottage deck.

I lived underwater, remembering
the inside of my mother,
floating in the sac
of her body, two layers,
amnion and chorion.
The first border between us.

Submerged, I could forget her songs,
songs about the desert and badlands.

To be unyielding was everything then.
Once I stayed below too long,
broke the surface, scales glittering,
to see her running
towards me, kicking off her high heels,
tearing off her dress, screaming
all the rawness of her love.

The Lost Herd

The lost herd that grazes
around my bed tonight tells me
birthmarks are tracks left by animals
moving through the dreams of pregnant women.
When they nudge my belly with their hooves,
I ask them if they left
that stain shaped like Australia
on my mother's left thigh,
and why they have come to me now, in mid-life
and childless.

Three Songs for Hands

On a summer evening,
we are five girl cousins kneeling
in our bathing suits
on the bedroom floor of the cottage,
playing *rock, paper, scissors*
to win the top bunk. Outside
the iron clang from the horseshoe pitch,
saskatoons changing colour like bruises.
All the way from Chippewa,
the tremolo duet of loon mates.
Again and again, we thrust
our hands into the centre,
paper covering rock,
scissors cutting paper,
rock crushing scissors.

*

Around my grandmother's
kitchen table, the women
in mother's knitting circle
hunch like birds over a nest
of needles filled with diamonds
for husbands' argyle socks.
They rip out stitches,
too much tension, or too little.
Their needles are small swords, click, slide
while the knitters unravel stories
buried deep in their bodies. At thirteen,
my breasts are still hard berries. I eavesdrop
from the pantry, wary of ripening.

*

Marriage has made my hands weep.
Inflamed, they erupt with eczema.
To stop scratching at night
I wear white gloves,
fake pearl buttons at the wrist.
I want the flawless hands
of the tiny plastic bride
on top of the wedding cake,
hands that reveal nothing.

Waiting for the Diagnosis

Until today I have avoided facials,
another kind of autopsy.

A stranger in a white coat
probes and strips, her arsenal

of creams, oils and sprays
scrub, cleanse, hydrate.

The promise of exfoliation—
of bones, skin, minerals,

to come off in scales or layers.
Hot towels on pores closed

tighter than the leaf
of my begonia before it slowly

unfurls, shiny green surface reaching
for the light, while the tender side

turns away from the world.
I press the insides of my wrists

against the table, the veins
a blue that could break, the pulse

jumping too close to the surface.

Kathy Sinclair

Kathy Sinclair was born in 1973 in Sidney, British Columbia, and grew up on the Saanich Peninsula. She studied writing and English literature at the University of Victoria. Through the Department of Writing's co-op program, she worked in a number of fields, including book publishing in Kelowna and government communications in Ottawa. In 1991 and 1993 she received the junior and senior creative writing awards from the BC Ministry of Tourism and Culture. Kathy Sinclair's poems have appeared in *Grain*, *Event*, and the *Fiddlehead*. She lives in Vancouver, where she works as a typist and tutor and serves on the editorial board of the *Capilano Review*.

THE LIVES OF GIRLS AND WOMEN:
POEMS THAT RING LIKE BELLS

When Kathy Sinclair was seventeen, she won a short story contest sponsored by the *Saanich News*. She knew then she was going be a writer—a writer of short stories and novels. However, in her first year of Creative Writing at the University of Victoria, Kathy was compelled to work in three genres: fiction, drama, and poetry. Although she had not been interested in poetry before, Kathy began to read the work of other poets and to explore the form herself. In no time she was hooked. Poetry became her first love.

I first read Kathy's poems in the summer of 1999, when I was giving a four-day poetry workshop for the Victoria School of Writing. Along with the other participants in the group, I was immediately struck by the maturity of this young woman's poems. In fact, we were all impressed with the clarity and sharpness of her imagery. Having been raised in more repressive times, a few of the older women in the workshop were struggling to tell their truths without obfuscation or self-censorship. In contrast, Kathy's poems spoke openly, with candour and intelligence. Her words rang out clear as a bell, a bell we all sat up and listened to with amazement and pleasure each time it sounded.

It is not surprising, perhaps, that Kathy began writing stories and moved over effortlessly to poetry. In many ways, her poems *are* stories—distilled stories about family, history, and relationships. Reading Kathy's words we find ourselves viewing the world through the keen eye of a writer, a writer who lovingly details an evening sitting on her bed upstairs in her parents' house, listening to the sound of her mother roasting a sirloin, and her father creeping from room to room, trying not to knock over trinkets or glasses. Kathy concludes "All the Dreaming" with a line that simply and powerfully expresses one of life's sad and beautiful truths: "Things won't ever be this way again."

Kathy's is a compassionate, encompassing vision. Whether she is writing about Nancy Drew's heroism, her grandmother's shame, or a sister's anxiety, she draws us into her poems and doesn't let go until the last word.

Why I Love Nancy Drew

Because she had titian hair
when I thought *titian* meant the hair of vikings,
giants of old.

Because she had a girlfriend named George.

Because in high school
she didn't give a fuck about the football captain,
prom dates or getting laid.
Because she liked to read and hang out with the girls,
instead of doing makeovers and manicures.

Because even though she lived at home with Dad,
I knew who wore the pants.

Because she cared most
about the things nobody sees,
knew where to touch the vase
to make the secret compartment open
and reveal a stolen necklace.

Because she followed her crazy hunches
while others followed their men,
because she searched out dark corners alone,
didn't scream at bats,
wasn't afraid to use a knife.

Because even now she tells me not to give up
until I find the missing piece.

Because she drove a small green Triumph.

Eggs

Every day now, I eat one
boiled at breakfast,
a warm and rubbery comfort.
I feel whole only
as it slides down my throat.

*

At Halloween
the neighbourhood boys threw
them against houses. One by one,
whole cartons whipped against the Nielsens',
the Huenes', the McCanns'.
When I woke the next morning
I looked out my bedroom window,
saw the orange sun rise like yolk
through shards of shell.

*

When I first learned
that even small girls
carry eggs inside,
I imagined the scene.
Inside my stomach: small sacks,
kept warm by tiny hens.

*

At nine
I carried my belly swollen
with the pride of an expectant mother.
I supposed the baby
would come by C-section,
sometime when I was asleep.
I never saw the child,
but my body felt
the loss.

*

Looking back I can't explain
why I practised breastfeeding
while the boys outside
toilet-papered the houses,
clenching and unclenching
their fists, eggs breaking
against those good solid homes.

The Bone, the Burn, the Fire

I. *Wanda Clara Corrine Simpson*

On rainy days in Brentwood
my mother's wrist gets tricky.
The small bones wax together,
make her drop things—tea cups,
books. I used to help her. She sensed
a storm from miles away.

All along she'd curse
the brother who pushed her into a ditch
after school for no good reason,
left a mark under the skin
that will never go away.

II. *Clara Bertha Elizabeth Simpson*

In photos my grandmother always faced right.
On her left cheek, a skin graft
told the story of a brother's cruelty.
He rocked his sister's cradle,
inching it closer and closer
to the oil stove.

When he wandered to their mother
in the pantry, canning peaches,
the baby's face was stuck to the open door.
It took a knife to pry her off—
no doctor on that island, help
an hour away.

III. *Bertha Elizabeth Brennand*

The small shop in Blackburn, Lancashire,
sold matches, candles, confections and wax.
CADBURYS, the outside sign read
above lead-paned windows.

Expanse of green, weighty
land of Hopkins, clumps of dirt
on the main path to the servants' shed.

One night my great-grandmother
was asked to fetch a package of cocoa
for baking the next morning. Her sister Freda
went with her to the basement,
carried a lit candle down the steps
while Bertha leaned for the jar.
And how it happened—the flames suddenly licking
the mutton sleeve of her nightgown,
an explosion—her sister slapping Bertha's arm
to put out the fire.

Freda tended to the wound with butter,
but these things, she said, take a long time to heal.

Sestina

Those days we knew we'd both be stars,
me tap-dancing on the hearth, my baby sister
and her voice of thin gold. Natural as birds,
"One more for the English relatives!" The burning
applause, transcendent. Perhaps in some sense
we both still carry those evenings, my cheeks glowing warm.

I remember the leather-faced clock above the warm
fireplace, its hands stuck at twelve. They pointed to stars
beyond the ceiling—suddenly I sensed
what lay beyond eye's reach. Meanwhile my sister
was already learning how to move like thin blue flame, burn
silently. Dinners she pecked at her plate, sad bird

over a salad without dressing. She watched as birds
careened just outside the window, nursed her warm
soda. How can one spend years this way, slowly burn
without being noticed, like Venus, the one bright star?
In dreams I stared at empty skies and saw my sister,
a constellation mapped out in six senses.

Mother shouted, *Eat, it's common sense.*
Even I couldn't see the wings of something, bird
or bat, shrivel within my sister.
All we wanted was to keep her warm.
Every night she watched the Stars
of Hollywood, Celebrities of L.A. burn

across the TV screen. Black-tie heroes burning
for the white-gowned women whom the senses

had blessed. One in red, sequins like stars,
waved to the crowds, her braceleted bird-
like arm a blur of wing. *How does she stay warm?*
Mother wondered, not seeing my sister

rise. Outside I could see the moon's pale sister
becoming more and more clear, a white cigarette burn
in dark fabric. I went to the kitchen to warm
a mug of milk, listened upstairs again for the sense-
less choke, the toilet flush. Instead I heard the glass bird
on the vanity fall, smash into thousands of tiny stars.

At night the starlight burns in my room, I think of you,
fall into a warm deep sleep. The birds are rare these days,
perhaps they sense the change, the change, my sister.

She Dreams Her Sister

She dreams her sister
dies, each time a different way.

One night she is jarring
applesauce with her mother when they get the call:
her sister has overdosed on sleeping pills.
She drops the phone,
slumps over the peels on the counter.
I always knew it would come to this.
Her mother hangs up the receiver
and wipes her hands on a plaid tea towel.
Let's finish this batch before we call your dad.

She looks out her window to see her sister's white coffin
perched on top of her car, covered in snow.
Pale blue light: a gold cross juts through.
She busies herself with needlework,
speaks to friends while facing walls,
then remembers in the midst of things
and cannot be consoled.
She calls her mother: *What do you want me to do*
with the body? burn? bury?

Awake, she cannot slice an apple without the knife
cutting across her own throat, cannot
walk ten steps over snow
without a shudder, cannot live
without calling home each morning
to make sure everyone's still
breathing

All the Dreaming

You're back in your childhood bedroom,
its jungle leaves encroaching.
Downstairs your mother roasts a sirloin.

At dinner you'll eat without thinking,
forget until it's too late.
Your father creeps from room to room

like a shadow belonging to no one,
trying not to knock over trinkets or glasses,
anything that might break.

With a warm mug you sit on your bed,
think of all the dreaming the pillows hold.
All that garbled longing.

Birds cry through the sounds
your mother makes: slamming cupboard doors,
the lids of pots. Not out of anger

but from being alive, it's her way
of praising. The silent tops of pines
have grown tall enough for you to see

from your window. In the distance
the observatory looks down from the mountain.
It isn't watching you.

Here on your bed you wonder
why you count only the arrival,
never the way there. As if in between

destinations you can act any way you please.
But for now there's this bedroom,
its greens and deep blues.

Downstairs your mother watches TV,
a spoon clinks in your father's cup of coffee.
Things won't ever be this way again.